Preservation Of Electronic Formats

Electronic Formats For Preservation

Preservation Of Electronic Formats

Electronic Formats For Preservation

Edited by Janice Mohlhenrich

Highsmith PRESS

Fort Atkinson, Wisconsin

Published by Highsmith Press
W5527 Highway 106
P.O. Box 800
Fort Atkinson, Wisconsin 53538-0800

The paper used in this publication meets the minimum requirements of
American National Standard for Information Science —
Permanence of Paper for Printed Library Material. ANSI/NISO Z39.48-1984.

Library of Congress Cataloging in Publication

Preservation of electronic formats & electronic formats for
   preservation / Janice Mohlhenrich, editor.
     p. cm.
     Includes bibliographical references and index.
     ISBN 0-917846-17-6 (alk. paper)
     1. Computer files--Conservation and restoration--Congresses.
2. Library materials--United States--Conservation and restoration--
Congresses. 3. Libraries and electronic publishing--United States--
Congresses. I. Mohlhenrich, Janice, 1956-   .
Z701. 3. C65P73 1993
025.8'4--dc20   92-38498
                                     CIP

  ISBN 0-917846-17-6

Contents

Appendices

Foreword

The papers presented at the 1992 WISPPR Conference describe a broad spectrum of research and development efforts currently underway in commercial, government, and academic settings. All describe attempts to extend the life of electronically stored data and to develop stable, cost-effective electronic alternatives for reformatting print collections. In the case of computer disks and CD-ROMs, neither the formats nor the equipment to read them were developed with permanence in mind. As a result, studies attempting to apply these or other electronic formats to the preservation of paper-based collections are dependent on resolving or at least overcoming the issues of permanency and access.

Although often diverse in approach, these papers describe certain common objectives:

1) To determine the long-term potential for digital image technology as a preservation and access medium.

2) To develop the necessary practices and protocols for adapting such technology to library and archival collections.

3) To improve existing technology with the goal of both determining and extending the life of electronic information for which there is no print analogue.

These papers provide a well-balanced survey of the research taking place at this time and underscore the progress that has been made in developing and testing the permanence of electronic scanning and storage of textual, numeric, and graphic data. Conference speakers also addressed advances made on the equally relevant issue of network access to electronically reformatted materials. The advances reported in these proceedings substantiate the viability of electronic technology as a preservation medium.

The difficulties yet to be resolved are of growing importance to all librarians and archivists whether they are faced with the preservation of their own paper resources or are charged with the acquisition and evaluation of data produced in electronic formats. The publication of these proceedings, therefore, not only provides a permanent record of the ideas presented at the Conference, but more importantly disseminates beyond the auditorium walls current findings relating to preservation and electronic formats, thus permitting a broader segment of the preservation community to review and evaluate the information presented.

The issues discussed at this conference will undoubtedly reshape preservation programs and priorities over the course of the next five years. This is only the beginning of a new era, an era in which technology offers an array of opportunities and challenges. Preservation options and practices are not static. Those who are concerned with preservation need to develop plans which are proactive and which incorporate new opportunities and new developments into existing programs. The information presented in these proceedings serves well to educate the preservation community and to stimulate discussion of the issues.

The WISPPR Planning Committee and its parent organizations, the Council on Wisconsin Libraries and the University of Wisconsin - Madison General Library System, are fortunate to have been able to bring together such an outstanding group of individuals directly involved in some of the most important electronic preservation research at this time.

ACKNOWLEDGMENTS

The following individuals deserve recognition for their roles in making the conference a success:

Cheryl Bradley and Angie Lueck, staff at WILS (Wisconsin Interlibrary Services) for travel, publicity, and local arrangements; Anne Tedeschi, consultant, for creating the brochure and providing information about WISPPR, and Andrea Rolich, Memorial Library preservation department, for assistance with plannning.

And finally a special thanks is due to Kathy Schneider, Executive Director of the Wisconsin Interlibrary Services, who has been with the preservation committee since its inception. Her encouragement and support have been a vital part of WISPPR's development.

Louis A. Pitschmann, Chair
Preservation Committee
Council on Wisconsin Libraries

Preface

Preservation of library collections is a much touted concern these days. The growing number of programs addressing preservation at ALA's annual conference bears witness to the interest in the field. All too often the concept of preservation is perceived as merely a glorification of book repair. This volume is a reflection of the importance of preservation as a holistic concept whose impact permeates every phase of the work done in the modern library from acquisitions to deaccessioning and every step and decision along the way.

The topics covered in these proceedings are wide ranging, yet each paper supports the others by adding just a bit more information, fleshing out details, suggesting related thoughts, or expanding on previously mentioned ideas. The purpose of this work is to educate the reader about the issues. In a time of fast changing technology, none can claim to have all of the answers. The only hope is to stay well enough informed that decision making is based on fact. It is essential that librarians have knowledge to contribute to shaping technology to meet needs rather than facing a position of adapting preservation strategies to technology imposed on libraries by vendors.

A long held maxim in preservation work is that it is necessary for conservators to recognize their limitations; to be able to recognize that their knowledge may not be sufficient to enable successful treatment of a given item. In such cases established wisdom is that it is preferable to do nothing rather than take a potentially damaging course of action. This same idea holds true in connection with electronic formats. The preservation community cannot in good conscience advocate adoption of technology if we do not first educate ourselves to the potential benefits and limitations offered by that technology. This responsibility for learning about new technologies and their ramifications for preservation devolves upon each of us.

WISPPR

Interest in preservation within the state of Wisconsin is strong. In 1987 a committee of those concerned with preservation was formed. Adopting the acronym WISPPR (Wisconsin Preservation Program), this adjunct to the Council of Wisconsin Libraries took on the charge of educating others about this important area of librarianship. WISPPR activities include presenting workshops statewide on a range of topics including book repair and disaster preparedness planning, exhibiting at the annual WLA conference, publishing a newsletter, and holding conferences.

PRESERVATION OF ELECTRONIC FORMATS & ELECTRONIC FORMATS FOR PRESERVATION

In the fall of 1992 at the WISPPR planning meeting, committee members gathered to discuss possible topics for workshops to be offered in the upcoming year. No one remembers exactly who first mentioned the need for information about the preservation of electronic formats, but our keen interest was apparent as we found ourselves talking excitedly about the questions each of us had concerning the topic.

- How will we preserve electronic journals?
- What is the future for microfilming?
- What do we tell people who seek advice about canceling paper index subscriptions in favor of CD-ROM products?
- How long will CD's last anyway? What are they made of?
- How should we store this kind of material?
- What is scanning all about, and what part will it play in preservation?

The committee realized that we had tapped a significant need for information, and began thinking and planning a conference, a WISPPR conference, to be held on the preservation of electronic formats and on electronic formats for preservation.

Members of the group were aware of the brittle books project being worked on at Cornell University and agreed that a speaker from that institution would be well received, as would a well-known figure in Wisconsin libraries to talk about local efforts to adopt new technology for preservation purposes. Like librarians nationwide, we looked for guidance and expertise from the Library of Congress and the National Archives. The encouragement and response we received from these institutions was gratifying. The research and development officers of some major commercial vendors in the preservation field were also eager to participate.

Anne Kenney, Assistant Director for Preservation at Cornell University, spoke about an ongoing project at Cornell to scan brittle books. Michael Pate from Marquette University described the start-up phase of a scanning project involving archival collections. Technical considerations for choosing electronic formats were explained in detail by Basil Manns, an expert in imaging technology from the Library of Congress. Mark Arps presented an industry update on the manufacture of CD-ROM products at 3M, where he works as marketing manger. Don Willis, Director of Advanced Technology at UMI explored the possibility of creating a hybrid technology combining scanning and high resolution microfilm. A number of issues recur throughout this work, including those identified by Anne Kenney: The lack of standards for the creation, storage, transmission, access and retrieval of digital images, and concern about the obsolescence of software and hardware. In Anne Kenney's words, the situation "cries out for collaborative solutions."

Our hope is that these proceedings can serve to spur communication about these issues. I invite readers to contact me, or WISPPR, or other state preservation programs to share thoughts about the ideas presented here. The ability to raise questions puts us closer to finding good solutions. I urge all readers to become part of the process.

ACKNOWLEDGMENTS

The work of preservation succeeds best when it is approached as a mutual concern touching all aspects of librarianship. The success of this conference and the creation of these proceedings reflects just such a cooperative effort. The excitement, enthusiasm and dedication of the WISPPR committee and the speakers who made up the program resulted in an excellent conference—well attended, well organized and thought provoking. Their vision led to an advance in knowledge in this field.

The experience of editing these proceedings has been educational. I appreciate the confidence of my fellow committee members in entrusting me with this responsibility, the cooperation of the contributors who all provided quality manuscripts (with just a bit of nudging needed), and the faith of Don Sager and Nancy Wilcox at Highsmith Press that this would be a useful publication. The help of Robert J. Sieracki in every phase of this project, from recording, to transcribing, typing, proofreading, and helping me stay calm in the face of an impending deadline is most gratefully acknowledged.

Editor's Note

Information given here may vary in the degree to which it replicates the talks given at the conference. Some papers may incorporate ideas that were discussed during the program. Others are the product of tape recordings that were transcribed and edited. In all cases this is true of the discussion sections. Uneven quality in taping required that occasionally a question had to be formulated when only the answer was audible. Every attempt has been made to provide the reader with complete and correct information. Any error or inconsistency should be attributed to the editing process, and not to the authors of the papers.

1

The Role of Digital Technology in the Preservation of Research Library Materials

Anne R. Kenney
Associate Director of Preservation and Conservation
Cornell University

In recent years there have been a number of prototype experiments in the use of digital techniques in library and archival applications, most notably at national institutions, including the National Library of Medicine, the National Agricultural Library, the Library of Congress, the Naval Research Lab, and the National Archives. These projects have resulted in important work regarding the capture, storage, and use of digital images. A current project, conducted at Cornell, builds on this foundation. For the past two years, Cornell University and Xerox Corporation, with the support of the Commission on Preservation and Access, have been collaborating in a project to test a prototype system for recording brittle books as digital images and producing, on-demand, paper replacements of high quality. The project goes beyond that to investigate some of the issues surrounding scanning, storing, retrieving, and providing access to digital images in a network environment.[1]

CORNELL/XEROX JOINT STUDY

From the very beginning, the cooperative aspects of this project have been instrumental to its success and have stemmed from a recognition that no one person has the expertise to do it all. Within Cornell, the collaborative effort involves Cornell Information Technologies and the University Library—I'm the co-manager in charge of the preservation related issues and Lynne Personius, Assistant Director CIT for Scholarly Information Sources, is co-managing it from the technical side. Equally important, this collaboration is apparent at the highest level:

both Stuart Lynn, the Vice President for Information Technologies, and Alain Seznec, the University Librarian, have given this project their fullest support which has been crucial to its success. Finally collaboration has extended beyond Cornell to the Xerox Corporation. Xerox does not have a history of including future customers in the design phase, so this project represents a departure for them as well as us. Lynne and I serve on the project development team which over the course of the past two years has met bi-weekly to discuss problems, possible solutions, timetables and future directions.

This project represents a real learning experience for both sides. It began with understanding each others' language. Xerox turned nouns into verbs with abandon, and they thought we spoke in letters instead of words, or we would both use the same word but with a different meaning—when they would speak of the need to "archive," I would first wince at the transformation of a noun into a verb, but also I've never thought of simply storing or copying something as archiving it. I remember one meeting early on which was very technical and almost incomprehensible—toward the end someone spoke of the need for "refreshment" and of something being "robust." My ears perked up. I thought, we're finally getting somewhere—glass of wine, some more genteel conversation—but that's not what they had in mind at all. Nonetheless, we have overcome communication barriers and this collaboration has resulted in the development of a scanning application that we feel is suited to the preservation needs of research libraries.

BRITTLE PAPER

The problem of brittle paper and the crisis this represents for libraries is well known. As much as one-fourth to one-half of the materials in this nation's research libraries require some form of preservation, and there are indications that the situation may be much worse in other countries. Exponential increases in book production have greatly exacerbated the twin dilemmas of preservation and physical access. Although bibliographic control of library materials has improved considerably over the past twenty years, much of the material the records represent is unusable or fast approaching unusability.

Archives, too, suffer the presence of brittle paper, but their paper-based collections are also endangered by unstable reproduction processes, inadequate storage and environmental conditions, and improper or frequent handling. Much of this material can be saved only by copying it onto a more stable medium.

At present, libraries and archives preserve the intellectual content of deteriorating originals through photocopying or microfilming. Both strategies fulfill important access needs. Photocopy benefits the local user by replicating the medium and format of the original document; however, the production of a single sound replacement does not contribute significantly to the national preservation effort that is based on the notion of reformatting deteriorating material once, storing a preservation master, and distributing copies on-demand.

Microfilm, if processed and stored in strict accordance with national standards, has an extremely long life and may be duplicated almost indefinitely with only minor loss of information. The technology itself is stable and the film produced may be read on any microfilm reader. While the high contrast film currently used is not totally acceptable for reformatting a large percentage of illustrated material or low contrast material, newer continuous tone films and stable color films are slowly becoming available that will improve this situation. As such, microfilm has been recognized as the preferred medium for copying, and forms the basis of a twenty-year brittle books program to preserve three million unique titles. This effort has extended to archival material and NEH and NHPRC are both supporting a number of archival filming projects. Nonetheless, microfilm is not a format favored by many researchers—it is inconvenient to use and does not convert to paper in a wholly acceptable fashion, and restricts the reader to a linear, sequential approach to material. It represents in a very real sense (pun intended) the return to the medium of the scroll.

Digital technology promises to combine the best features of both microfilm and photocopy. It offers advantages in terms of ease of further reformatting and duplication, image capture enhancements, and the opportunities for improved access and space savings. Unfortunately there are some real drawbacks to the technology as well, which center on the lack of standards for the creation, storage, transmission, access and retrieval of digital images; and because it is an emerging technology, the rate of obsolescence in hardware and software. The problem is not so much that an optical disk will only last ten or twenty or even one hundred years, but that one won't be able to "read" the disk in five years. Little wonder then that funding agencies and institutions alike are reluctant to support preservation efforts that rely on digital technology.

DIGITAL IMAGE TECHNOLOGY

I'd like to take a minute to define what I mean by digital image technology: A digital image is the electronic copying of scanned documents in image form.

Charles Dollar of the National Archives calls it "an electronic photograph." The text contained in these digital images is not converted to alphanumeric representation at the time of scanning—these are not text files but images of actual pages—as such they are not searchable. The present capabilities of optical character recognition or keying in are inadequate or prohibitively expensive for capturing both the information and the presentation of the original document, which is critical when replacing rapidly self-destructing material.

The creation of digital images does not preclude the use of OCR capabilities. In fact it represents the first step in that direction—the scanning of paper copies to which Character Recognition software can be applied, for the purposes of creating indexes into the digital images or ultimately when OCR capabilities improve, to replace the digital images.

PRELIMINARY PROJECT CONCLUSIONS

With that definition of digital image technology in mind, I'd like to present some of the conclusions about the use of digital technology which we have reached in this project:

1. First is that 600 dot per inch scanning and printing results in a high quality paper replacement for brittle materials. It also represents the highest level of resolution currently achievable in a production environment.

2. The ability to create microfilm directly from digital files exists today.

3. Very soon, digital technology will come to represent an affordable alternative to microfilm and photocopy for reformatting brittle material.

4. Digital technology has the potential to revolutionize access to material, and to change radically a repository's role in making resources available.

5. A meaningful evaluation of digital technology's impact on use requires the development of a carefully chosen and expanding digital library of thematically-related documents. For this reason, digital technology could have broad implications for the selection of material to be preserved.

6. Much work remains. This project has raised many more issues than it has addressed about the capture, storage, transmission and retrieval of digital images. This is an area that cries out for collaborative solution.

PROJECT GOALS

Quality

Our first concern with using digital technology centered on quality. Digital technology offers several important advantages over both photocopy and microfilm. First, it has the potential to create a higher quality reproduction of a deteriorating original than does conventional light lens technology. Because a digital image is an encoded representation—essentially a string of ones and zeros—there are certain advantages to copying a page digitally. The image can be reproduced over and over with no resulting loss of quality. With light lens processes, there are discernible differences between second and subsequent generations of an image.

Moreover, a digital image can be manipulated in a number of ways to improve image capture. For instance, Xerox has developed a windowing application that enables us to capture a page containing both text and illustrations in a manner that optimizes the reproduction of both. With light lens technology, one must choose which to optimize: text or illustration. In preservation microfilming, the current practice is to shoot an illustrated page twice, once to highlight the text and the second time to provide the best capture of the illustration. A digital image can also be edited and density levels adjusted to remove underlining, foxing, or stains, or to increase the legibility of faint documents. On-screen inspection can take place at the time of initial setup, and adjustments made prior to scanning. This ability has reduced substantially the number of rescans required in quality control. Obviously in producing a replacement copy, decisions must be made as to how much enhancement is desirable or affordable.

A primary goal of the Cornell/Xerox Joint Study has been to evaluate the paper output printed on the Xerox Docutech, a high speed printer that produces 600 dpi pages from scanned images at the rate of 135 pages per minute, which is faster than most mainframe printers. While lower resolution scanning can produce satisfactory copies from crisp, high contrast modern documents, many of the deteriorating volumes in this project contain irregular features typical of the production typography and printing techniques of the past century and a half or are heavily illustrated with very fine line drawings and halftones, or are in languages such as Japanese where the build up of characters comprised of varying strokes is difficult to reproduce at lower resolutions. A surprising number contained annotations or mathematical formulas which were really challenging. The mathematicians insisted, for instance, that we not turn pluses into minuses in the scanning process! The 600 dpi copies successfully capture most of these publishing challenges to represent faithful and legible reproductions of the originals. As the copies are being printed on paper that meets the ANSI standards for permanence, and the Docutech printer meets the machine and toner requirements for proper adhesion of print to page, as described by the National Archives, the paper product is considered to be the archival equivalent of preservation photocopy.

An example of the quality achieved in this project can be seen in figure 1. This is a small part of the print on-demand copy of the 1911 Rede Lecture on the Steam Turbine. The original contains halftones, line drawings, and illustrated text.

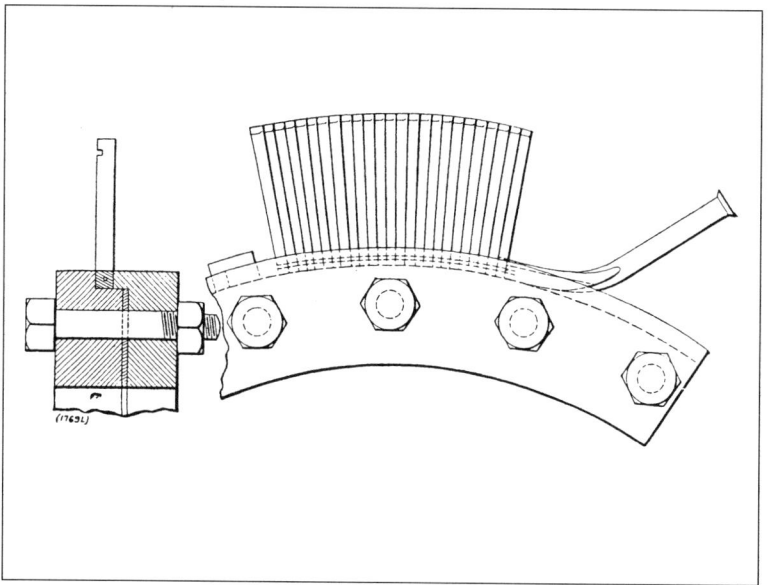

Figure 1: Systems of Blading from *The Steam Turbine*

We have compared the capture capabilities of scanning to photocopy for a standard test target. Photocopies we produce for preservation, using a Canon 8580, are produced both at the regular setting and using the photo setting. The regular setting does a good job of capturing text and lines, but a terrible job with the photograph. The photo setting improves the illustration but sacrifices the text.

Figures 2–5 compare the quality of 600 versus 300 dpi scans of a test target. They were scanned on the same machine at the same settings of filters, thresholds, etc. and made use of windowing to capture the photo and the gray scale at the top while capturing text as high contrast black and white. In figures 2–3 we want to show the differences in the quality of the scanned text. The text from the 600 dpi version isn't quite as sharp we can get from photocopy, but it's not that much worse—the two point text is still legible—and certainly the overall capture is superior. The 300 dpi sacrifices text—the two point text is illegible and the four point text breaks up. (We have reproduced the scans at 150% to make differences clearer here. Complete test target is reproduced in Chapter 6.) Figures 4–5 compare the 300 and 600 dpi scans of the photograph. The overall superiority of the 600 dpi scan is especially evident in the photograph. I am able to discern eleven levels of gray scale when viewing the whole target of the 600 dpi copy. More dramatically, the photograph of the 300 dpi version is very grainy, similar to wire service photographs, whereas the 600 dpi is more faithful to the original.

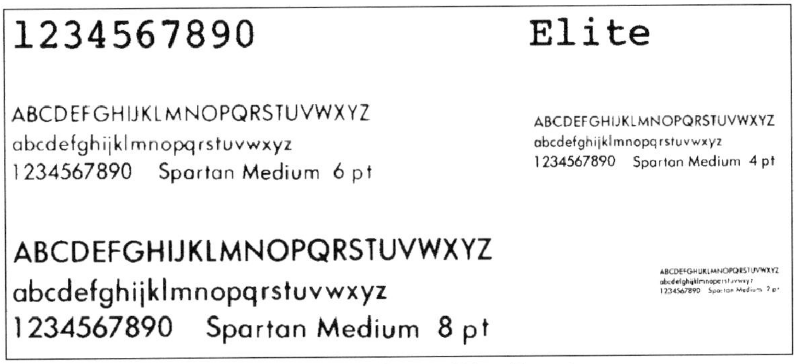

Figure 2: Type Sample from 300 dpi Scan of Test Target

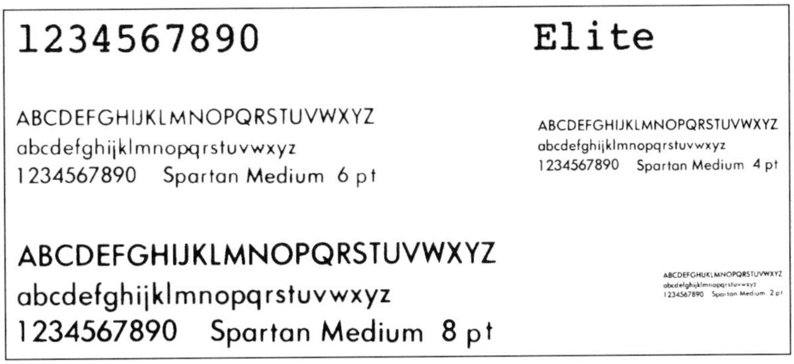

Figure 3: Type Sample from 600 dpi Scan of Test Target

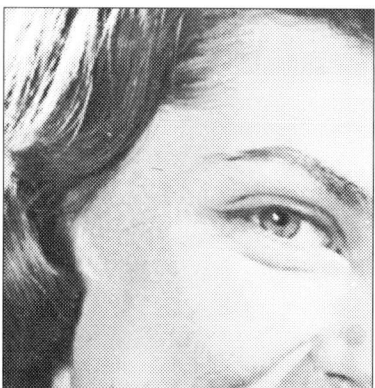
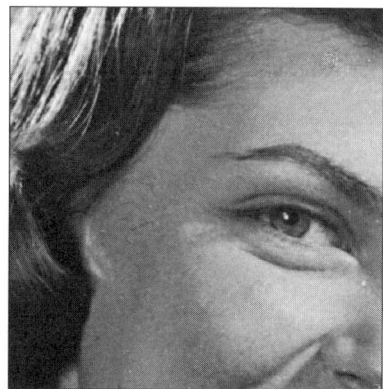

Figure 4: Photo Sample from 300 dpi Scan of Test Target

Figure 5: Photo Sample from 600 dpi Scan of Test Target

While sample text targets are useful in comparing various processes, it is important to note that they represent just one sample of scanning. A higher level of quality is achievable through enhancements. It's also important to state that the Cornell Project investigated the quality achieved with binary scanning only. There is great promise in gray scale and color scanning, and the advantages/disadvantages of the various approaches need to be examined. Scanning resolutions and file formats can represent a complex trade-off between time, file size, fidelity, on-screen display, printing, and equipment availability. Our study had as a primary emphasis the production of printed facsimiles that were largely black and white text in a timely and cost-effective manner.

With binary scanning, large files may be compressed efficiently and in a lossless manner using CCITT Group IV Facsimile compression. In our project, we achieved a 40:1 compression ratio. Gray scale scanning results in very large files and compression using JPEG is much less economical and results in a lossy compression method: compressing and decompressing results in subtle change to the image. It appears that while binary files produce a high quality printed version, other combinations of spatial resolution with gray and/or color hold great promise. Gray scale also can represent an advantage for on-screen viewing. For instance, on a low resolution screen display, two bits of gray at 100 dpi will be better than 600 dpi or 300 dpi binary. The advantage is lost, however, when the on-screen image is enlarged. Much experimental work is needed to define the various trade-offs based on the type of image, volume of material to be scanned, costs of production, and use of the digital images.

The Cornell project has focused exclusively on published material. Next year, we will turn our attention to archival material. We are proposing to conduct a feasibility study with the big eleven comprehensive research libraries in New York State (NYPL, Columbia, NYU, NY State Library, Rochester, Syracuse, and the four SUNY campuses at Albany, Buffalo, Binghamton, and Stony Brook) to determine some production benchmarks and image capture capabilities for a wide variety of archival material held in their collections. Each institution will choose up to two hundred pages of material—from handwritten letters, to thermofax copies, letterpress volumes, to photographs, drawings, blueprints, broadsides, and reports for scanning and digitizing at Cornell.

The emphasis will be on quality and the development of default settings to capture typical archival material, such as the wide array of photographic and copying processes present in our collections. The institutions will be asked to compare the scanned paper version to photocopies of the material and to the originals in terms of quality and acceptability as replacements. They will be guided in their evaluation by a set of criteria developed at Cornell with the assistance of image scientists at Xerox. Each will prepare a written assessment of the use of digital technology and its current capabilities as a reformatting medium for a variety of archival and manuscript materials. The institutions will also receive copies of the digital files for experimentation in the areas of access and use.

Production of Microfilm

Our second finding of the Cornell/Xerox project involves the production of microfilm from the digital files. To date, the digital files for one book containing straight text, halftones, line drawings, and illustrations embedded in text have been used to produce sample film using an electron beam recorder developed by a company called Image Graphics, Inc. The recorder is configured for standard micrographics applications recording of high-resolution digital images and gray scale. The resulting film is faithful to the image capture of the digital files, and while the text cum image pages are superior to that of light lens film, the resolution readings for 600 dpi are not as high as standard microfilming; again, I was able to read the 5.0 test pattern. It may well be necessary to use a higher dpi system, or a combination of high resolution and gray scale, to reach the exacting standards for image resolution set for preservation microfilming by ANSI, AIIM, RLG, and others. It could also be argued that the micrographics standards are best suited to capturing straight-forward published text since they only measure resolution, the number of line pairs per millimeter, and density, the darkness of the exposed film; and have not taken into consideration image capture.

Certainly with archival material the issues of handwriting and various media pose challenges beyond resolution and density. A microfilm copy can be perfectly within acceptable ranges yet represent a very poor reproduction. I would argue that the standards defined for light lens technology are not totally transferrable to a digital environment. Moreover they are based on defining quality for the preservation copy—the copy that gets stored in the mine shaft, not the use copy. We made a printout of the technical target that had been microfilmed according to preservation standards and it was by far the poorest representation of the original. But making this case will be a long uphill struggle. We will continue to investigate this issue over the course of this year.

The Yale Project to convert large numbers of microfilmed volumes to digital files will result in valuable comparative data on quality and cost. The advantage of creating microfilm is that it can serve as the primary backup and as the preservation master. The digital files would then become the print or production master, and the service copies could be paper, film, optical disks, magnetic tapes, or on-screen displays. There are decided advantages in being able to separate the medium for preservation from the medium for storage and use.

Production

A third goal of the Cornell/Xerox project involves the development and testing of a moderately high resolution production scanning workstation. To date, 1,000 brittle volumes (approximately 300,000 images) have been scanned. The resulting digital files are stored and used to produce hardcopy replacements for the originals and additional prints on-demand. While this project is an experimental one and initial costs are high, our findings suggest that scanning technology offers an affordable means for reformatting brittle material. A technician in production mode can scan 300 pages an hour when doing single sheet scanning, a necessity when working with brittle paper. Subsequent iterations of the software are expected to increase this rate of production.

Over the course of three months, we conducted a time and cost study for scanning and found that an average 300 page book takes about an hour and 40 minutes to scan. This figure includes time for setup, which involves keying in primary bibliographic data, going into quality control mode, defining the page size, establishing front to back registration, and scanning sample pages to identify a default range of settings for the entire book—not dissimilar to functions performed by filmers or those preparing a book for photocopying. Once setup is complete, the scanners move into production and essentially scan "blind" the rest of the book. There is very little quality control performed during production scanning, although certainly the technicians can stop and view the image, dot by dot on the screen. The final step in scanning involves rescans, which happily are few and far between: well under 1% of the pages needed rescanning.

In addition to technician time, we have costed out the equipment (amortized over four years), the costs of refreshing or recopying of the digital files every four years and the cost of printing and binding a paper reproduction. It comes to a little under $65 per 300 page volume if we include 30% for overhead—quite competitive with photocopy vendors. This cost will rise only slightly over the decade as the costs of storage and refreshing decline to offset the rise in labor and finishing. These figures also assume that there will be no increase in production, which will almost certainly occur, and that the files must be recopied every four years. This time will lengthen as standards for data transfer and physical media are developed and implemented. Photocopying which is a much less dynamic technology, will not see similar declines, only increases.

If one were to inflate photocopying costs by a modest 3% per year, the difference between the two processes would continue to widen, with photocopying being 20-25% more expensive by decade's end. With scanning, in addition to the paper facsimile, one is also left with the digital files, so subsequent copies of the book can be produced for a fraction of the cost of photocopy and readers are afforded choices in the form of use copies.

One of the most exciting and promising aspects of using digital technology is that it may provide the electronic means for a library preservation effort to pay for itself. If a brittle books program includes the means for disseminating reprint facsimiles or books that are in demand by libraries and researchers alike, the initial investment in image capture can be recovered and used to preserve additional, but low demand, books. An economic model for a self-sustaining program is based on the idea that more hardcopy versions of books will be sold than microfilm and that for every X number of copies sold of a title, another book can be preserved. The model also assumes that for some titles, significantly more copies than X will be sold and that for many titles, no copies will be sold.

NETWORKING

Digital technology has the potential to revolutionize access to material and to change radically the library's role in making resources available. Within our lifetimes we will see a shift to the development of a digital library. In the not too distant future, readers will be afforded choices in the way they use information. Once an item has been scanned, they will have the opportunity to "browse" an index to the item or the actual page's image at their workstation and to place an order for a paper copy without leaving their office or dorm. By relying on national networks, it will be possible to transmit digital files from one institution to another. The use implications are that for the first time, preserved material will be more easily accessible than the original: in fact, multiple access will be possible for the first time. Readers will be able to use the resources of a number of libraries and archives without physically going to them. The digitized documents themselves could come to represent a special electronic collection which no institution owns but all may use.

Some have even argued that the network itself will become the library. This concept presumes a willingness on the part of libraries and archives to make their collections accessible beyond their four walls and traditional interlibrary loan channels. It is a clear understatement to suggest that this will require a significant change in the access policies of many institutions. Nonetheless researchers will soon expect information regardless of its origin or location, and librarians and archivists will have to provide a seamless transition to it. They could spend as much time accessing information not under their control and redirecting researchers as they do serving their own collections. Reference service in the future will consist of providing access to distributed collections and distributed users.

The anticipated changes in access and use are predicated on making the digital images available across networks and providing mechanisms for accessing those files easily and quickly. The Cornell/Xerox project has from the beginning provided a network connection (See figure 6.) between the scanning workstation located in Olin Library (upper left) and the Xerox Docutech (lower left), located in the Information Technologies Center one half mile away, over Cornell's TCP/IP network.

Cornell and Xerox are now in the process of converting the remaining portions of the system from a stand-alone one to a compatible network environment. This system provides a means of storing and accessing digital files from an Image Server (upper right), consisting of an optical jukebox and a UNIX workstation. The image server enables the scanning technicians to transmit digital images for storage on 12" optical platters in the jukebox and to recall images stored there for viewing or replacement as needed. Records for the 1,000 volumes have been entered in both RLIN and Notis, Cornell's local sys-

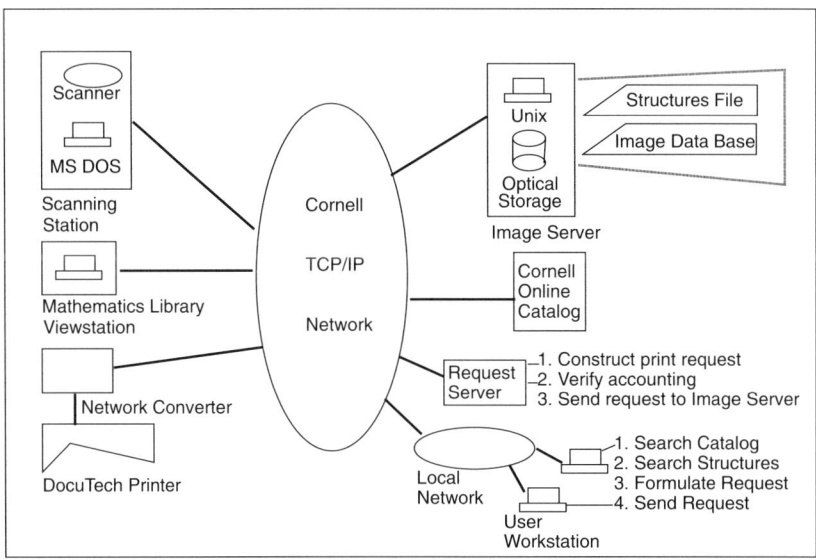

Figure 6: View of User Access to Digital Images

tem. Readers will be able to log into the request server (lower right), being developed at Cornell, which will provide them with the capability to request printed copies of documents stored on the jukebox.

The next step will be to provide researchers (lower right) with the digital images themselves. In the Cornell/Xerox project, scanned images are being created as TIFF images and compressed prior to storage using Group 4 CCITT compression, both of which represent de facto standards in this field. Translation to other formats governing image data is possible. For instance, an image file can be converted from group 4 to the more common group 3 fax standard, which governs the transmission of images by fax machines. Some preliminary experiments in this area have demonstrated this feasibility. To date, image files have been converted and "read" by Image Graphics for film production. They have also been viewed on an Apple MacIntosh, an IBM PS/2, and a NeXT workstation and made available via File Transfer Protocol to those outside Cornell.

This spring, Cornell demonstrated the networked system at Net92 in Washington, where the images stored on the jukebox in Ithaca were accessed and reviewed. Cornell has received additional support from the Commission to provide national access to the growing digital library. Over the course of the next year, Cornell will develop an image conversion server that will permit images to be delivered to a variety of hardware platforms, such as the Apple Mac, IBM PS/2 and the Sun workstations, and therefore to scholars outside library buildings and beyond the Cornell campus.

Remote access to digital images presumes a national networking infrastructure that can accommodate the transmission of massive data at high speeds. The files for digital images are large. Even compressed, the image files in our project average from 60,000 to 80,000 bytes per page. Transmitting a significant number of digital images would overwhelm moderate to low capacity networks. The National Research and Education Network (NREN), named in the High Performance Computing and Communications Act recently signed into law, will consolidate the collection of TCP/IP networks now known as the Internet into one high speed, high capacity system. It is predicted that the increasing capacity of such a national network will keep pace with the demand for the timely transmission of an increasing volume of large digital files. But this is a big "if." In the immediate future institutions must consider such issues as transmission delays, traffic jams, and the slowdown at the institution level. Going across the NREN may be fast, but gaining access for those last 100 feet locally may be problematic.

At Cornell, the library is connected to the TCP/IP network, which is ethernet (10 megabits/sec) by an omninet (1 megabit/sec). This fall the campus is being wired with fiber (FDDI network) which will increase traffic to 100 megabits/sec. The question of speed of retrieval and user patience will have to be explored carefully. Of course, even delays of several minutes are insignificant when compared to the time it would take to retrieve the physical object itself.

DOCUMENT STRUCTURE

In addition to making digital files available in a network environment, there must be a means for accessing those files easily and quickly. Critical to all of the system design and networking configuration for capturing books is the document structure. A document is made up of two discrete components. First, there is a collection of images, each representing one page of a book. Second, there is a document structure database that links a collection of images together to define the document.

The overriding principle that guides the definition of the document structure is that the correlation between images, and any page numbering printed on the originals, will be retained. The second principle for books is that the user must have easy access to those self-referencing portions of the original. The table of contents, the index, list of illustrations or other pages that provide entry to the text should be tabbed for easy use.

It is our belief that the creation of the document structure for a given book should be kept as simple and straightforward as possible. The two principles, to provide retrieval by original page numbers and access to self-referencing sections, are relatively easy to implement by the scanning technicians. More complete indexing would require additional time and a higher level of subject expertise, thus increasing the cost of initial capture.

In the digital environment, images may be viewed as part of more than one structure. Ultimately, for example, artificial collections can be assembled and annotated by defining a new document structure record describing text files and digital images that were originally part of several documents, located at different institutions. The ability to produce customized documents offers scholars new opportunities for research and publication, but will pose challenges in the area of copyright, privacy, and authenticity. We anticipate working with other universities in more fully developing this structure to accommodate the networked concept of a document. It seems clear to us, however, that the document control structure will be a critical component in making digital images accessible to researchers.

Developing access into archival collections is both more problematic and simplified. Collections don't come paginated with self-references and they must be processed to be used effectively. Yet at the same time, archivists are used to providing, through inventories and finding aids, more detailed access to collections than is provided for books through the bibliographic record. Increasingly, our finding aids are machine-readable and so are easily made available in a networked environment. The challenge for archival collections will be to move beyond the indexing of distinct collections to providing intellectual links regardless of where the material is located. Our finding aids in the future must be interactive, not collection bound or repository bound. Much work remains.

LOCAL ACCESS

Another component of the Cornell/Xerox project is the development of a public viewstation. A networked prototype is located in the Olin Library, where users can access the digital images for material located on the optical jukebox and ultimately from jukeboxes around the country. A reader will be able to access simultaneously material from a variety of repositories. The viewstation was created by Xerox, with input into the design by a committee of Cornell librarians and computing professionals. It is designed to assist a reader who is searching the collections to choose material for use.

The quality of the on-screen image is quite acceptable for viewing and browsing. We've been experimenting with providing 200 dpi images on a screen with 110 resolution. For extended reading, a user will want to request a print-on-demand or the 600 dpi digital images that are stored on the optical jukebox, or if only a few pages are needed, to generate a local print. This work-station represents the first step in providing a level of access that approximates looking through books in library stacks or comparing the contents from different collections. The ability to provide an electronic surrogate for shelf browsing, or collection review, will be essential if the digital library is to become a reality. Although no real user studies have been conducted, the viewstation was located in the Mathematics library for six months, where readers were able to access 50 mathematics volumes. The math librarian reported steady interest on the part of faculty, staff and students in the use of the digital books. He also noted that there has been no use of the microfilmed versions of similar material that has been collected by the library for the past twenty years!

SELECTION OF MATERIAL

While the prototype for changing to a digital library is being developed, it seems clear that means of access and use may not be substantially altered if only discrete items are digitized. Digital technology could have broad implications for the selection of material to be preserved. To date, library preservation projects have focused primarily on microfilming important deteriorating works. It has mattered more that all items selected were considered worthy of preservation and had not already been filmed than how they related to each other. Funding agencies have required that the microfilm be cataloged as a means to make this material available, but the primary benefit from improved bibliographic control has been to avoid duplicative filming efforts rather than enhancing access. Certainly institutions have chosen thematic approaches to preservation microfilming, and have cooperated with one another to preserve their combined holdings in particular subject areas, but these projects have not substantially altered the use of this material. Digital technology could assist libraries in adopting an approach that is more archival in nature where there will be a shift to viewing the value of material in a context and in relation to other material. It should also encourage archival repositories to take a more global view of preserving and making available their collections by providing readers with unprecedented opportunities to view material not just in one context but a variety of contexts.

Digital technology could well turn the preservation/access issue on its head, with access becoming the more dominant of the two. This shift could depend in large measure on the availability of related sources and the development of a corpus of material in digital form. I believe that a substantial digital library must be built before we can begin to understand fully how the availability of images online will affect research. As collection development librarians and archivists determine priorities for digital preservation, they should consider not only the value and physical condition of the material, but also how selected items relate to other items in their collections and at other institutions. Because inter-institutional cooperation can result in the development of a special digital library, accessible across networks, selection decisions can be guided by a consideration of the potential uses researchers may make of this material. It seems probable that the use of digital technology to preserve and make accessible deteriorating research materials could alter traditional methods of selection for preservation.

CONCLUSION

In conclusion, I'd like to emphasize several things from a library perspective. The impact of digital preservation on libraries and archives will be significant in a number of ways.

1. We will begin a shift from reliance on microfilm and photocopy to digital preservation, although this shift will take place over the course of this decade. This transfer will follow other trends already underway: we have already seen the analog record replaced by the compact disc; newspapers are now transmitting photographs in scanned digital form; one half of the phone service in America relies on digital technology; and more recently the U.S. has embraced a digital standard for High Definition Television as opposed to the analog standard proposed by Japan and Europe.

2. Digital technology will also affect the way we make material accessible, over networks instead of through our doors. This will require libraries to assume a closer cooperation with information technologies which will become the custodians of an increasing percentage of our holdings as they already have become for our bibliographic information networks. We must build mechanisms for control and preservation of those materials maintained only in electronic form and out of our direct care.

17

3. If we move away from replacing book for book brittle material on library shelves or paper for paper in our archives to providing network access and prints on-demand, we need to work hard to develop an electronic browsing mechanism and to develop connections between the online catalog, indexes and finding aids to material, and the material itself. This will obviously have ramifications for technical services and reference functions.

4. Finally, the development of an international digital library will also affect collection development and access. As geography becomes less of an issue, libraries and archives could move further along the continuum from ownership to providing enhanced access to information. The late twentieth century could see the fulfillment of Erasmus' sixteenth century vision of "…building up a library with no limits other than the world itself."

In sum, the use of electronic technology will affect a whole array of library and archival functions, causing us to integrate more closely our activities. Among the challenges ahead for research institutions are: to develop evaluation criteria for testing of technology to meet library needs; to define repository requirements for suppliers of technology and services, and to encourage their development of such services; and to create inter-institutional mechanisms to address issues such as storage, selection, standards, access, distribution, copyright, privacy, and use. We need to gain an understanding of how the relationship between researchers and resources may change with the shift to digital technology and network access. These issues must be faced collaboratively if research institutions are going to move toward the use of digital technology not only for preservation but a whole array of other library and archival functions as well.

Notes

1. The Final Report of the two-year study has been published: Anne R. Kenney and Lynne K. Personius, "The Cornell/Xerox /Commission on Preservation and Access Joint Study in Digital Preservation Report: Phase I (January 1990–December 1991) Digital Capture Paper Facsimiles and Network Access." Commission on Preservation and Access, Washington, DC, September, 1992.

Discussion

Q. Obviously Cornell has really come a long way with this project. It really makes me wonder if there is any point in continuing to produce microfilm. If digital technology is the wave of the future we may be investing in obsolete technology. There is of course the issue of backup still to be considered.

A. I think your first question really said it all, whether we really need to produce preservation microfilm from the file. I think that we can look to what is happening to our online catalogs. We don't have any card catalog in the sky backing that up, yet we've learned to live comfortably with the idea that this stuff is really well maintained, cared for, and backed up and we need to take that analogy and move it to the digital library as well. In our cost analysis we have built in the cost for refreshing and maintaining and storing those digital files over time and if you were to look at the issue of the cradle to grave costs of any kind of preservation method you will find, I think, that digital technology may well provide the cheaper alternative in the long run. It costs a lot to keep a book on the shelf, and to circulate it, and to send it through interlibrary loan and get it back. With digital technology you can skip the whole step of preserving that book on the shelf, and when you have an ILL request you just send them off a relatively inexpensive paper copy with no cares whether it comes back to you.

Q. Wouldn't it be more cost-effective in the long run to create very high resolution microfilm, when you consider the need to have a reliable backup for this information?

A. We backed away a little bit from that initial assumption. It is just too early to tell, and when we found that the resolution of the test targets for digitally produced microfilm were not as high as light lens technology, we started looking at alternatives to backup. Pat Battin has argued that we're using microfilm as an interim measure and it really is not an access vehicle at all, it's a preservation medium and that ultimately we'll take all that film and create digital files for people to access. If you look at the costs of producing something through microfilm and then creating digital files, to the costs of scanning from paper and then producing microfilm I thing it's going to be cheaper to do the latter than the former.

Q. How much will the technology need to advance, is it possible from the digitized copy to produce microfilm?

A. Sure.

Q. Once information is scanned, are we locked into an either/or situation with the technology of adopting either digital output or film as our choices?

A. One of the nice things about digital technology is the tremendous variety of outputs—paper, film, on-screen, optical disks, CD-ROM, magnetic tapes....

Q. How soon will outside users be able to access the information being scanned in your project and what sort of interface will be required?

A. The work that is being done at Cornell this year is to provide an image file server, I think that's what it's called, that will enable someone to access that digital library from a Mac, from an IBM PS/2, from a Sun workstation.

Q. You said that data is refreshed every four years. Is that time frame critical? Does the data break down in that length of time? Isn't refreshing data that often going to be very expensive?

A. We chose the year four because that's what they've been doing at Cornell with some of their data in their archives. When you copy a bitmap representation, a binary scanned document, you don't lose anything in the copying. It creates a faithful copy each and every time you do it. It's a string of zeros and ones, and if a zero looks a little like .2 it will be a zero, and if it looks like .9 it will be a one, so copies are very good. We actually believe that the costs of copying and refreshing will be more economical than maintaining the material on its original disk as the costs of storage and access decline dramatically as they have historically over the past decade or so.

Q. I'm still not clear about the idea of refreshing. Why would you need to do this so often?

A. The need for refreshing is based on the assumption that the medium itself is fragile and that there will be hardware and software upgrades in technology that may result in your not being able to read it ten years down the pike because the equipment and software has progressed so rapidly in that decade.

Q. Wouldn't it make more sense then, to choose a format, disk, magnetic tape, or whatever, that offers more stability? It seems like things will be lost with all this copying.

A. The physical disk, or the tape itself is also fragile. Even if you had one that could last a hundred years, at this point I wouldn't put something on an optical disk that lasted a hundred years and then stick it away somewhere because I wouldn't be able to read it. You know, the 1960 Census is only readable on two machines now, one in the Smithsonian, and one in Japan.

Q. I'm interested in more details about the jukebox you described. Who makes that, and how many disks can it accommodate?

A. It's a Xerox supplied proprietary jukebox, it holds 12" optical platters, I don't know how many, maybe 64 of those, I think we're getting 60-100 books per side. In the course of this project we have had direct access through the public viewstations to the optical disks on the jukebox, but we're shying away from that because Cornell, particularly, has students that like to crack codes, and security, and release worms, and since we are vouching for the authenticity of the digital images, we don't want someone to go in and muck with them, or have anybody change them in any way. So we are preparing a buffer image server which will speak directly to the jukebox. Workstations will speak to it, and it will take the message off to the jukebox.

Q. We've been looking into the scanners now available on the market for use in a project at our library. What costs are involved with the scanning equipment Cornell is using in this project, and is it now available on the market?

A. Our scanning system is a prototype and Xerox does not have it on the market yet. I think they're looking at, for the PC, the local storage device, the software, and the scanner, something like $20,000. Don't quote me on that exact price and call up Xerox and order!

About the Author

Anne R. Kenney is the Associate Director of Preservation and Conservation at Cornell University. She received her bachelor's degree from Duke University and her master's in history from the University of Missouri at St. Louis. She also has a master's in library science from the University of Missouri at Columbia. She received training in preservation and book binding at the Missouri Botanical Garden Library.

She joined the staff at Cornell in 1988 where her administrative duties include the commercial binding office, the brittle book program, microfilming and the scanning project. She is currently project director of Cornell's NEH funded Southeast Asian microfilming project and co-project director of the Cornell/Xerox joint study on digital preservation funded by the Commission on Preservation and Access. She's also a member of the Cornell University task force on digital technology and visual images and the university's committee on electronic publishing.

She is currently Vice President/President Elect of the Society of American Archivists and is a member of the committee on text and image preservation at the Commission on Preservation and Access.

2

The Marquette Electronic Archive

Michael B. Pate
Assistant Director for Public Services
Marquette University

TEXT IN THE LONG VIEW

I would like to make some preliminary observations on what I would call "text in the long view" before beginning with the primary topic of this paper. Any of you who have experienced Harvey Wheeler will have had a taste of this already. Harvey was one of the original thinkers of the concept of virtual books, virtual libraries, and virtual universities. Communications, writing, and text production are all closely a part of human culture, wrapped up in it, so to speak, and this is not the proper setting in which to fully discuss this—nor do we have time, but we should still be aware of the progression from clay tablets to the Internet.

Ever since man first drew and scribbled on cave walls, we have had a tremendous drive to "write." Now in this age, we face new opportunities of imaging and writing in an electronic environment. We are again in an overlap stage in this process, just as in 1000 BC writers were using stone, clay and wood tablets while at the same time the newest application of papyral scrolls were just emerging. It would be interesting to listen to the comments that were made in those years about this new "volume" treatment— "books" that were not on a hard surface. Again in 300 AD, the "new" codex form of the book was just being put into use in Rome. For many, many years, scrolls existed side by side with "books"— codex volumes. The convenience of this newest improvement became obvious in a relatively short time—a couple hundred years. Paging was certainly easier than scrolling.

The biggest innovation to accept for those who were attached to the handwritten book either in scroll or codex form came when movable type and multiplication of volumes became possible. A book was just not a book unless it was inscribed by hand. Only those with money and power owned them. Through printing, the physical object—the pages, the writing, the encasement—was becoming less important than the information it contained. By many this was seen as a serious degeneration of basic learning skills and a threat to the established order. Now it was possible to distribute books far and wide. Everyone who could learn to read could have and use books with relatively little cost. The hegemony of the few, particularly the priesthood and legal/government establishment had an important foundation in the limited access to written text. The power base could change. We are so far removed from this time of change that our common mind has forgotten the issues.

We face other issues now and we are again in a time of change and overlap. Electronic formats now besiege us and those of us in this business of learning, transmission, and preservation of knowledge are grappling with new problems of economics, access, and permanence. The physical objects persist but now we have other ways to read, store, and transmit. Now, for $40 it is possible to own and read the works of Shakespeare, the Bible, the Koran, the Book of Mormon, 18 historical documents, the teachings of Confucius, the Buddha, and eight of the most outstanding works of fiction in western culture all on one CD disc and with the use of the Sony Data Discman, have a personal "Library of the Future."

Most of the famous works that are on this disc are also available in at least one location in electronic text, available for transmission to a personal computer over the Internet. Electronic text is proliferating as we speak today.

THE MARQUETTE ELECTRONIC ARCHIVE

So what is Marquette doing in the midst of this quiet revolution? I intend to give you a detailed description of our work to date, but as a quick overview let me say that we are still in a prototype stage of converting some of our open, special collections that fall under the general field of Catholic and Native American interests. We are still seeking funding to prepare full text files, using standardized markup and indexing protocols for the following: the published writings of Dorothy Day, a co-founder of the *Catholic Worker* newspaper and the movement of the same name; the Marquette finding aids to the Bureau of Catholic Indian Mission records, other Catholic Indian mission collections, and the published work, *Guide to Catholic Indian Mission and School Records in Mid-west Repositories*; the index to the post-1960 publications of the United

States Catholic Conference (USCC) and to the full text of selected out-of-print USCC publications.

Our intent at this time is to prepare these files for permanent residence on a Marquette VAX computer. They can be used here, locally, applying the Data Retrieval, (DR) TextDBMS search software or requested in whole or in part by anonymous FTP to any remote site with an Internet connection. In these cases, the files will carry text tagging. An online user would also be able to use the files with the DR search protocols. We will, of course, list the availability of the Marquette Archive in the appropriate network and published sources. We have just begun an investigation of the application of Hypertext to the project, but this decision is some time away.

The paper will describe how we came to the decision to proceed, the process of preparing grant applications, a description of the prototype project, and some reflections on possible impacts of such a project.

A PERIOD OF TRANSITION: THE MARQUETTE UNIVERSITY SETTING 1990

This section of the paper, although not vital to a review of the electronic text project will describe the university dynamics behind the project and is one example of how this Jesuit university plans its future, which in the end relates to how it provides access to and preservation of its resources. Tuition income is the major source of the Marquette operational budget.

In October of 1990, a new president was installed at Marquette University. From this beginning, President Albert DiUlio, a priest of the Society of Jesus, has taken a special interest in the library, its relations with the University, and with the larger academic world. His inaugural address took the community by surprise when he identified new directions that he hoped could be initiated by and through the library. He was and continues to be particularly interested in expansion of the library, its electronic support and extension of its collections and services. This announcement came at a time when, as we all know, colleges and universities have been especially hard pressed to support their libraries at even a "normal" level.

As the new year opened a "library of the future" concept unfolded. Unprecedented encouragement from the Jesuit and vice presidential levels identified the field of text scanning and digital technology as ways in which Marquette could move into future technologies. A vision of a library of the future is focused on ways and means of moving Marquette toward a more significant contribution in a wider world of scholarship—taking positive initiatives in areas where Marquette could show its historical interests. Keep in mind that the Marquette library staff had just "come down" from five years of successful planning for and implementation of an integrated, online catalog. But it was not only the library for which there were interests of instilling a new vision. The School of Education and its Literacy Clinic have submitted proposals to move toward a closer relationship of support and service to an ailing Milwaukee Public School system in the PIVOT Proposal. A Family Studies Center has been established. All departments of the university have been invited to participate in a massive rehabilitation/redirection for the upper Wisconsin Avenue part of the city—the Marquette neighborhood. This is formally known as the Campus Circle Project, for which Marquette is seeking Federal assistance, besides several millions of dollars from local businesses, the hospitals and the City.

So the new ventures of the library represent only one set of proposals in a much larger program of change that is now beginning to take hold across the university and in its Milwaukee setting. There is definitely an interest in making a name for Marquette beyond its traditional regional university connotation. The visions of the new administration have, of course, been watched both with favor and criticism and a fair level of tension at the operational levels since new money to start these initiatives has not flowed down from on high. To a library that has not had a history of aggressive moves toward untested, high-tech programs, nor been encouraged to identify and seek extramural support, the interest in finding and developing new programs has come as a shock. Promises of additional university funds for collection enhancement, equipment and staffing have been a factor in gaining library cooperation and support of the new interests.

In February of 1991 the library administrative staff set upon the task of identifying what Marquette Libraries have to offer the world that would be worthy of an expensive investment in digital technology and distribution. Even though the university administration has been aware of the new opportunities for text scanning, networking, and electronic-based scholarship in general, there has been a naive understanding of what is necessary to make a worthwhile, credible contribution in this new field. Ironically, but probably rightly so, the library staff have been tempering this development while some of us gain understanding—I would hesitate to say "expertise." The staff has been very careful to identify only those materials that have a demonstrated history of use by active researchers. There has not yet been much new money for the project, nor has the university had the reserve to hire in leading experts. Staff time has come entirely from the existing positions and it has been up to the library to define how we should proceed.

There certainly has been a clear mandate to proceed in looking for outside funding! The example for this was provided by the corporate vice president when he successfully attracted a local software firm, Data Retrieval Corporation to donate its DEC/VAX based indexing and searching software to the university at the cost of maintenance only. The library project will give that company, Data Retrieval, the opportunity to show off its wares in the academic setting where it has not previously had customers.

MARQUETTE UNIVERSITY LIBRARY SPECIAL COLLECTIONS

I believe that with good sense, the library administration identified collections in the Special Collections and University Archives as those that will have interest at the national level in such new applications.

Founded in 1961, this department reflects the spiritual, philosophical, and scholarly strengths of the university as a Catholic and Jesuit institution. The department actively collects: 1) the records of the university, its faculty, staff and students; 2) records and papers which document the involvement of Catholic organizations, movements, and individuals in promoting social change in the United States, including change within the Catholic Church; 3) records which document the involvement of Catholic organizations among Native Americans and records relating to Christianity in Native North America; 4) records and papers relating to the history of Jesuits and Jesuit institutions in Milwaukee, Wisconsin and the Midwest; 5) the records and papers of organizations and individuals involved in Catholic radio and television; and 6) the papers of Marquette alumni who are artists, writers, popular entertainers, broadcasters, journalists, or politicians. Containing over 8,550 cubic feet of archival and manuscript collections—roughly 12,000 linear feet—Marquette has developed an archival program of national scope and significance.

The department has a strong public service orientation and serves a large and diverse clientele. During the past four years (1988–92) research activity averaged 4,932 uses annually. In 1991, 6,308 uses were recorded. Non-university records which attract the most frequent and persistent use are the Dorothy Day/*Catholic Worker* Collection, the Catholic Indian Mission records and the J.R.R. Tolkien manuscript collection. Nearly one-half of all users are from outside the Marquette campus, consisting of the general public, alumni, and students and faculty from other institutions.

The department has a depository responsibility along with the Memorial Library Reference Department for the publications of the United States Catholic Conference (USCC) and the National Conference of Catholic Bishops. A staff member in the Reference Department (Phillip Talmage) just completed an index to these publications since 1960. The USCC published this in March of 1992. The index is in ASCII text, and it along with selected out of print publications from the USCC files will be part of the electronic archive.

GRANT PROPOSALS

The process of proposal writing has helped us sharpen our thinking about what we might do, how we would do it, and to what end. The first deadline involved a proposal to the National Endowment for the Humanities (NEH) on August 30, 1991. The library staff who were working on this project were not ready for the level of activity and intensity necessary to prepare such a proposal, nor had we established the contacts with the NEH that are so important in such a large project. The university encouraged us to move on it anyway. One member of the library group, Chuck Elston, head of special collections and archives had been involved in earlier NEH proposals and has been a reviewer of other NEH projects, so we at least had some experience in our camp. From the beginning, we looked upon the proposal process as a means of definition and a learning experience, and we were not surprised to hear (on May 23) that our NEH proposal would not be funded.

We went on to do two other major proposals, these to the Department of Education under Title II. The first, due on October 28 under the "Strengthening Research Libraries" program and the second due January 17 under the "College Library Technology" program. As of this writing, neither of these have reported out.

The process of proposal writing relates directly to any work we would try to do in the electronic text and preservation fields, since neither are adequately funded by our university   All of our proposals have been approached as a team. An archivist, authorities on the special collections that we described in the proposals and technical consultants in scanning and microcomputer applications have all been involved. Representatives of Data Retrieval have assisted in preparing sample databases and searches. During the last two proposals we made special efforts to seek letters of support from scholars who know the collections and to establish an advisory group to assist us during the two to three year period the grants would cover. All of the normal requirements of grant application procedure have been addressed with painstaking detail including strict adherence to the instructions and specifications, complete descriptions of the collections being included, with information on past use, descriptions of our work procedures, schedules, equipment specifications, cost sharing with our staff and the software provider, exhibits of articles about the collections, letters from researchers, annual budgeting and methods of dissemination to the interested research community.

The prose of the applications was written and revised carefully, especially following the NEH proposal when we were very short of time. The consultation that was necessary during the drafting stages was very important in clarifying our thinking and this process itself was a major factor in helping us define what we think we can do if the project is funded. Even though we had guidance from the Marquette Development Office and budgeting assistance and final preparation done in the Office of Research Support, the library participants have been the major researchers and writers of the proposals. This will be important for us to remember as similar opportunities for outside funding become available. It's a lot of work and with yet unknown results.

BROWN UNIVERSITY, WOMEN WRITERS PROJECT AND THE TEI

Sometime during our early investigations of scanning and electronic text, I was introduced to the HUMANIST List from Brown University on the Internet. This was an eye opener for me, and through HUMANIST, I discovered Elaine Brennan of the Women Writers text project, Michael Sperberg-McQueen and Lou Burnard of the Text Encoding Initiative (TEI), Anne Kenney of the Cornell project, Michael Hart of the Gutenberg Project, the Oxford Text Archive, Michael Neuman of Georgetown University, Eric Dahlin of US Santa Barbara, Susan Hocking of the Princeton/Rutgers Center and a host of others actively working in the field of electronic text. An invitation came up to attend the first North American Workshop on the Standard Generalized Markup Language (SGML) and the TEI. I attended this in July of 1991.

The background provided by this workshop was a major boost in providing the confidence level to me and through me to our group to go ahead with our project. Further reading and discussion about TEI, using the Internet, and explaining our interests to our colleagues at Marquette have taken us on a new tack that has contributed directly to the formulation of the project and provided more credibility to the grant proposals we would be working on.

THE DOROTHY DAY PROTOTYPE PROJECT

This is the "how we do it" section. We have had few models, and even though in writing our grant proposals we envisioned the procedures we would follow, all of this has been conjecture. None of the working group, nor anyone we could find locally had been involved in the preparation of "permanent" electronic text. Few staff or faculty at Marquette knew anything about SGML tagging and none had heard of the TEI guidelines at the time we began our investigations. Certainly, a number of faculty had used the Destin scanner at the Computer Center, and a few had transmitted or received full text files from colleagues over the Internet. This situation is changing now, but only over a period of about 18 months. Reservations and sign-ups are now required to use the new Apple OneScanner, but all of this, except our project are for personal teaching and research activities.

We have designed a set of procedures to follow in handling a small body of text from Dorothy Day so that we can learn how to proceed. The prototype includes Day's writings in the first six issues of the *Catholic Worker*, the first chapter of her book, *From Union Square to Rome*, and an article from the 1938 *Commonweal*, "The House on Mott Street." We will use the text from these sources to test our questions and procedures and to create a small searchable file for our advisory group to use on disk or by direct access on the Internet.

Dorothy Day was, and through her writing and life example continues to be, an important influence in Catholic social action. She and Peter Maurin founded the *Worker* in 1933 and with it a movement that continues to inspire. Her words, sentences, and themes from the early pages of this one penny newspaper still resonate with compassion and love for the poor and the destitute, for peace and against war, for responsible use of this earth, for respect for one another, and generally for the unapologizing example of the life of Christ. Day was a pacifist and anarchist and defended both positions. Her influence as a journalist and as an important human being persists and for these reasons we believe that her writings will continue to be an important part of this genre.

Besides the recognized importance of the work of Dorothy Day and of her writings and the likelihood of immediate use, there are a number of other reasons why we have chosen this sample for a prototype of the larger project. The text of Dorothy Day represents a challenging form for scanning and tagging. We have access to the entire original file of the *Catholic Worker* and to all of her books and articles. Phillip Runkel of the Marquette Department of Special Collections and Archives is the nationally recognized archivist of the Catholic

Worker movement and holds an in-depth knowledge of the life and writings of Day, and therefore becomes the natural guide in our decisions in the use and preparation of this text.

We have begun with the first six issues of the *Worker* and follow a series of steps that were only just begun in January of this year. The following represents a typical sequence of activity:

1. Phillip prepares two sets of photocopies at 25% enlargement from an issue of the *Worker* for all of the articles that he determines have been written by Day. Through experimentation we discovered that the enlarged text works better for scanning. We also begin cutting out all of the column divider lines, head line text—any designs on the paper that will confuse the scanner. An entire article is kept intact on the same sheet when possible.

2. Phillip marks one set of the photocopies for in-text tagging. He then sends both sets—the one that has been tagged and the "clean" photocopy to Keven Riggle in the Science Library, our staff member on the project who is most familiar with scanning, microcomputer use, and text tagging requirements.

3. Using the OmniPage OCR software on a MacIntosh MacIIci machine, Keven scans and corrects from the clean photocopy of the text using an Apple OneScanner.

4. A working file is created, checked for misreads and the Spellchecker is run. Preliminary header tagging is applied and the file is saved as a Mac ASCII file. Scanning on the text so far is running about 99.0–99.5% correct. The file is then transferred to the VAX mainframe so that it can be downloaded into the DOS environment for SGML/TEI tagging. In the newest version of the Data Retrieval software we will be able to apply tagging in the WordPerfect environment. The DR software will have a shell for direct tagging.

5. The file is downloaded onto a DOS machine and the header tagging is applied from a saved program along with minimal structural tagging since this is all that is required for the use of the DR TextDBMS search software. This completed step is saved as a separate file.

6. Keven then prepares a file for full, detailed tagging based upon Phillip's in-text marks for topics, words, names, quotations, and other judgements about what is important to have designated in the text. Structural tagging had already been used from the previous file. It is this file that will

become independent from our in-house search software and would be made available for remote use. Tagging at this time is only being applied to words that come directly from the text.

7. The process so far creates three separate files:
   a. one corrected file in ASCII with no tagging
   b. one with minimal tagging for use with TextDBMS
   c. one with complete tagging.

At this stage of our work all of these are simply numbered files based upon the issue and date of the *Worker* or article source. There has been no merging or external organization applied. This must all come later.

8. A printed version of the "a" and "c" files are run for Phillip to proofread. Phillip sends back a marked text for correction or any additional tags. Keven adds these and the text is proofed again.

Certainly, this is a complex process, not helped by the fact that we do not have all of our working equipment in one location and by the fact that we work from the Mac to the DOS environment. Our proposals for funding include two complete DOS stations with attached scanning equipment and software. In this way one station will be for scanning and correction of text and the second will be for tagging, printing, and proofing.

Even so, the various steps require detailed concentration and time commitments by the working staff. We have no designated staff for the project at this time. It will be possible to involve student labor, especially at the text preparation and scanning stages, but so far we are still learning the steps ourselves. The proposals describe a position that will be responsible for the computer and tagging process. Phillip will remain as a project archivist.

SIGNIFICANCE OF THE SGML/TEI GUIDELINES

It might be well to ask why we bother to apply text tags at all. I don't know if heat is still being generated over the use of the Text Encoding Initiative or not, but the appearance of a recent exchange in the *Times Literary Supplement* indicates that there may still be a fair amount of misunderstanding still prevalent about the TEI and the application of TEI conforming text tagging.

One of the primary purposes of the *Guidelines* (read "developing standards") *of the Text Encoding Initiative* is to allow the easy interchange of text between individuals at different sites who may be working in different computer environments. Also, the TEI sets forth a set of common terminology in the creation of electronic text and guidelines for moving text from one application to another. Standard Generalized Markup in the framework of TEI will become the "convention" for application-free text. It won't be necessary to prepare text in multiple forms if the TEI is followed. The TEI will also allow the use of common terms and tags in the retrieval of portions of text. The tags stay with the text wherever it goes and tell it how to behave.

We are still at an early stage in using the encoding *Guidelines* and the major movers in this field are now preparing the next version of these developing standards. In our project, we are still learning the various applications of tagging under the TEI guidelines.

ELECTRONIC TEXT AS A PRESERVATION MEDIUM

There are others imminently better qualified than I am to address the broader aspects of this topic, so I am concerned here only with the implications for our project.

In the case of the *Catholic Worker*, the electronic text offers another medium for preserving the fragile, challenging text of the newspaper format. The earliest issues of the paper are already yellowed and brittle. The bound reprint, by Greenwood Press (1970) constitutes 4 volumes in their *Radical Periodicals* series, but covers the *CW* issues only from its beginning in 1933–1961. The microfilmed version, available from University Microfilms, Inc. covers the period 1973–1986, now incomplete but this will be brought forward. We also own a microfilmed set provided to Marquette by the Catholic Worker that begins in 1934. The microfilmed editions of the *Worker* offer the expected advantages and disadvantages of a 35mm filmed original—a compact, scrolled text. It is still assumed that the master for the microfilm is the "permanent," "preservation" copy. The microfilm is often difficult to read or copy. Photographs in the newsprint have not photographed well. Some are black boxes in the text.

In this case, the electronic text, with sufficient backup copies becomes an alternative, more accessible version of the original text only, but again only an imperfect image of the newspaper text as is the microfilmed version.

We are seeking permissions to include the seven published books by Day and have already gained this for her articles in the *Commonweal*.

There is no serious "preservation" problem with the finding aids to the Catholic Indian mission records. The aids are typewritten and can be easily reproduced in photocopy version. These too can be microfilmed if that appears necessary.

The publications of the United States Catholic Conference do present a preservation problem. Many of these are out of print, and some are important and will have continuing research interest. Many libraries, church offices, or schools have discarded the earlier, now "unneeded" publications since they do not address current issues. An electronic version therefore, offers a clear option for preservation purposes. So far, there has been no decision by the Conference to reissue their earlier material although we have discussed some cooperation with the Conference on this topic.

Electronic text as a preservation medium requires a new set of responsibilities, particularly of the producer of that text. Keeping the computer format, be it disk, tape, or whatever "fresh" and usable, applying the most current operating program and even more basic, keeping the text in the most widely applicable machine language/format—which happens to be ASCII now, all fall under this responsibility. Related to this of course is understanding the necessity of a match with the most widely used hardware and network platforms.

THE MARQUETTE ELECTRONIC ARCHIVE AND THE SCHOLARLY COMMUNITY

Without the vision and encouragement of new leadership at Marquette, we would undoubtedly have continued working undisturbed with text on paper, microfilm, and the known electronic based services, placing our energies into the expected fields of library resource sharing but with primary emphasis upon "our own" academic community. The project has certainly caused us to think more seriously about the needs and perhaps yet unarticulated interests of a broader future community. Is the project a harbinger of forms of library resource sharing that will eventually fall upon even the smallest institutions with unique, special holdings? It has been particularly uncomfortable for many staff and faculty to think of Marquette in this role. Specifically, let me address the more immediate and defensible positions for the individual collections included in the project.

In the case of the Dorothy Day writings, the electronic archive will offer a sophisticated "concordance" to a difficult, scattered, original text that is largely without indexing at this time. The wide variety of her work now in many sources, aligned with uniform tagging under one rubric will offer the opportunity for establishing relationships that are presently not easily determined. The entire corpus can be searched and read as one work of many parts. When a search engine such as the Data Retrieval text retrieval software is applied, words, phrases, themes and concepts can be examined in context.

In the case of the Catholic Indian mission records finding aids, the project offers a publication and distribution medium that does not yet exist. The presence of these collections at Marquette will become more visible than has been possible with the printed, published handbooks, directories, and guides such as *Subject Collections* by Lee Ash or the *Dictionary of Special Collections* or *A Guide to Special Collections in the OCLC Database*. Use of an electronic finding aid with an external search engine applied provides access to the details of holdings, interrelatedness, and comparisons that are not now possible with the printed guide. Any direct access to an archival finding aid offers considerably more depth of description than does the MARC format for the OCLC archival cataloging entry. Remote use of the finding aid coupled with machine searching opens entirely new choices for a researcher who may not be able to visit the institution, or who when visiting may be short of time.

Both the Dorothy Day writings and the records of the Catholic Indian Missions have known investigators who often return. There is a documented trail of new users of these collections. Interest in the publications of the United States Catholic Conference is less well known. Librarians, faculty in seminaries, and some diocesan officers who have been surveyed tell us that the entire output of the USCC needs to be given better bibliographical control. This applies especially to the Post Vatican II materials. In this case, our project will provide both a retrievable finding tool and as we and the USCC staff identify publications of lasting merit, an economical means of reproduction, distribution, and preservation.

IMPLICATIONS OF THE MARQUETTE PROJECT

In our grant proposals, we have pointed out that we may be one of a small number of institutions—perhaps the only university special collection department, that is offering access to full texts of parts of its collections or finding aids. Using the Internet for this may also be a first. We are still considering other mediums in which to offer the electronic text. Our approach is an obvious use of scanning technology both for digital storage and transmission or storage and use of images of the documents themselves. This application is becoming common practice in the office filing environment. Why should it not be so in the archival and research community?

We know some of the obvious answers to this question that relate to frequency of use versus the cost of handling the often massive collections of original text. Much of this text is in manuscript and/or fragile condition, but perhaps the greatest percentage of it is in printed or typed form that is easily scanned. The access to and use of collections that are of manageable size could certainly be facilitated by these new technologies.

In summary, let me identify three primary advantages in the use of electronic text in the archival or special collections fields:

1. The value of the original material will be enhanced. The "added value" of wider scope, organization, indexing, and transferability enhance and broaden the use of any given body of documentary material, even though the material may have been in some print or published form.

2. Multiple electronic formats will represent another alternative for preservation of the original material. This will become more important as the technology becomes more reliable and better understood by greater numbers of professionals in this field.

3. The process of preparing text in electronic form will allow the materials to be shared beyond the walls of the library or other collection setting. This is not necessarily a requirement in every text project, but it may become one of the primary goals. In the future library setting, institutions may hold more obligation for this means of resource sharing which is beyond the present limitations of photocopying. The expectations on the part of researchers will move in this direction.

My archivist colleagues tell me that entire sets of original documents and related pieces of a given collection frequently are of varying size, format, media, durability, and legibility and must be examined together and in close proximity to the original materials in order to make accurate assessment of the whole and of each part. The context of each piece is important in this situation and no known application of technology could duplicate the real thing. The virtual reality in this case is not yet possible. This may be true now. It may not be true in the future.

In spite of these limitations, we believe that the problems we are addressing in the Marquette project can and should be addressed in similar archival and special collections shops. If funded, perhaps our investigations and other similar ones can be replicated in other settings.

Bibliography

Electronic Text in the Library and Research Setting

Basch, Reva. "Books Online: Visions, Plans, and Perspectives for Electronic Text." *Online*, July 1991, V.15, no. 4, pp. 13–23.

Brown, Heather. "Standards for Structured Documents." *The Computer Journal*, 1989, V.32, no. 6, pp. 505–513.

Garrett, John R. "Text to Screen Revisited: Copyright in the Electronic Age." *Online*, March 1991, V.15,no.2, pp. 20–26.

Hart, Michael. "Project Gutenberg: Access to Electronic Texts." *Database*, December 1990, V.12, no. 6, pp. 6–9.

Lynch, Clifford A. "Text Encoding Initiative." *Bulletin of the American Society for Information Science*, June/July 1989, pp. 15–16.

Oxford University Computing Service Archive. *A Short List of Machine Readable Texts Held at Oxford*, November 1991.

Pate, Michael B. "Preparation of Electronic Text—Report from a Workshop." *New Tech News*, Council of Wisconsin Libraries, Madison, WI, September 1991, pp. 1–3.

Pankake, Marcia. "Humanities Research in the 90s: What Scholars Need: What Librarians Can Do." *Library Hi Tech*, 1991, V.9, no.1, (Consecutive Issue No. 33), pp.9–15.

Rose, Steven J., David G. Durand, Elli Mylonas and Ellen Renear. "What is Text, Really?" *Journal of Computing in Higher Education*, Winter, 1990, V.I, no. 2, pp. 3–26.

Smith, Joan M. "The Implications of SGML for the Preparation of Scientific Publications." *The Computer Journal*, June, 1986, V. 29, no. 3, pp. 193–200.

Sperberg-McQueen, Michael and Lou Burnard (editors). *Guidelines for the Encoding and Interchange of Machine-Readable Texts* (Draft: Version 1.1, October, 1990) Text Encoding Initiative, Chicago and Oxford, 1990, Association for Computers and the Humanities, Association for Computational Linguistics, and Association for Literary and Linguistic Computing.

Wiberley, Stephen E. "Habits of Humanists: Perils and Pitfalls." *Library Hi Tech*, 1991, V.9, no. 1 (Consecutive Issue no.33), pp. 17–22.

Discussion

Q. How long would it take you to scan, tag, and completely produce online an entire book using the Data Retrieval software you've described?

A. I don't know, we haven't gone that far. We've done article length. If the article is from the *Catholic Worker*, where there might be a four column article; and the whole process of scanning that article, assigning tags, and proofing it once, may be a four hour process.

Q. I'm not familiar with the tagging process. How involved is that, and what percentage of the total time spent in preparation on a document is in the tagging stage?

A. Tagging is difficult. We're least able to predict what's involved in that. We're also least able to convince the people who potentially could give us money at the local level to do this, that this is a significant activity. I don't know if others of you have discussed the tagging responsibility in electronic files with any funding sources, but with sources at your own local institutions, it becomes a question of "Why bother?" Why not just prepare straight text? Why not offer the text as it comes off the scanner? As soon as you offer it off the scanner and it goes into another environment than your own computer environment, you risk loss and damage to important configurations of the text. That's the reason for doing that.

Q. The materials you've mentioned, the newspaper and the finding aids— are they only text, or are there images that you have to be concerned with in this project?

A. There are certainly photographs, there's artwork in the *Catholic Worker*...the text does not depend on the illustrations and we've purposely chosen text that we do not have to be concerned with as far as images. We're not now doing anything about the illustrations. We do have microfilm backup copy of the *Catholic Worker*, which is available from University Microfilms, as are a number of other sets from the *Radical Periodicals*, but the microfilm sets do not do well with the images or the art work that's in the text. Our sets of the microfilm have many black boxes where there are photographs or illustrations.

Q. So after you do the tagging and use the Data Retrieval software, what you end up with is a digital file?

A. No, you don't have a digitized file unless you couple that with the optical character recognition software. That has to happen at the level of the scanner. The scanner functions through the OCR software.

Q. How does the software that you're using and the end result of it differ from the files being created at Cornell in their scanning project?

A. The Cornell project uses a software base that's, I don't know if it's using an OCR software...Our object is to end up with straight digitized text so we have to be sure it's been corrected. We're not creating an image—the Cornell project is creating an image. We're creating a transferrable, digital text.

Q. You use something, a software in addition to the Data Retrieval?

A. Yes, we use a software called Omnipage.

Q. Does the machinery have a built-in spellchecker type device, or are the proofing and correcting you talked about done manually?

A. We proof it directly with the original text. It's human checking. An example project some of you may know of, the Women Writer's Project at Brown University is recreating in digital form the writings of women through the centuries that are either out of print or very inaccessible. They have six levels of proofing using student labor involved in that part of the process, comparing one-to-one with the original text. There's a tremendous amount of human labor involved in creating digitized electronic text.

Q. I can't believe it's feasible to do this if you have to have such a tremendous amount of human labor involved. At what point do you decide it's just not worth the effort?

A. I can't, we've been advised if we can't get to a level over 95% accuracy, it's not worth attempting to scan it. It's better to key it. We're running about 99%, so we figure it's worth it. In any given column of text from the *Catholic Worker* we may see eight to ten missed characters, wrong characters—the speller gets some of those, the automatic spelling device, but a lot of it is simply watching for the signal on the screen that tells you you've got a misread character, and then you correct it by hand. So that process is somewhat laborious, although if you run close to 98% or so, it's still worth doing.

Q. There must be some way to increase the original level of accuracy to eliminate some of the tedious proofreading. Is it possible to utilize OCR software this way?

A. No, good thought though. The project I referred to by Chadwick Healey, the *Patrologia Latina* which is a classic collection of the Latin fathers writings, that entire set, multiple columns the size of the Encyclopedia Brittanica, over 200 volumes, is being keyed by hand, because the text of the original volumes does not scan well. It's being keyed offshore and it's being produced. The first CD product from that project will be available to look at at the American Library Association meeting this summer. I can purchase that set in either CD or electronic tape format. I think the price ranges now between $50,000–60,000. It's a one time project, it will not be coming out with supplements. Once it's done it will be done. But that's from a set that finished publication in the early 1900s. I guess we've got to look at projects of this sort and say, "What's in it for whom?" In this case, they're selling it as a commercial vendor. There will be a number of libraries that will mount projects of this type for materials that either the preservation interest or access interest is such that the electronic format is a viable choice.

About the Author

Michael Pate is the Assistant Director for Public Services at Marquette University. He earned a B.A. in History and an L.S. from Western Michigan University. One of the things that he is very much interested in, and involved with, is automation. He was the chairman of the Marquette University Library automation committee that selected and implemented the computer system; he's served as a consultant to other libraries in their automation planning and selection process; and he is a former chairman of the Advisory Committee for the New Technologies Information Service, which is part of the Council of Wisconsin Libraries. He's been instrumental in implementing Marquette University's electronic archive project.

3

The National Archives and Electronic Records for Preservation

Fynnette L. Eaton
Branch Chief
Technical Services Branch
National Archives and Records Administration

The purpose of this paper is to discuss the issues confronting archivists and librarians as they attempt to preserve information that is stored in electronic media. My goal is to make these issues comprehensible, and while not suggesting final solutions, explain the issues in such a way that you are no longer traumatized by the seemingly insurmountable problems posed by electronic records.

By providing a general outline of what is meant by preservation and then describing the similarities and differences of preservation activities between the more traditional paper-based records and electronic records, I hope to put into clearer context the universal issues posed by the preservation of archival records. After this general introduction, I will then discuss in greater detail the physical and intellectual preservation of electronic records, providing examples of the efforts employed at the National Archives to achieve these goals.

In this paper, I will use the term preservation as it has been defined by Anne Kenney in her introduction to the special issue of the *American Archivist*, the journal of the Society of American Archivists, which was devoted to the topic of preservation. She defined preservation as "… all activities associated with maintaining materials in their original form or some other format…" and distinguished conservation from preservation by defining conservation as relating to physical or chemical treatments.[1] The premise of this paper is that the basic goal of preservation is to assure that records in archival custody, such as the National Archives, survive as long as possible, as long as it is legally necessary, or as I have said elsewhere till the end of this Republic.

The importance of preservation has become generally accepted by the larger community, as evidenced by the increasing number of articles published, library and archival meetings devoted to this topic, and by the existence of a national commission and office within the National Endowment for the Humanities committed to this activity. This concern for the preservation of our national heritage is no longer limited to the paper records. Photographic, sound recordings, motion pictures and yes, even computer created or electronic records, are subjected to the same concern for preservation.

Electronic records are probably the least understood by the larger archival and library community as far as their preservation requirements are concerned. What is interesting is that many of the preservation policies that are constructed around attempts to prevent deterioration are just as relevant to electronic records as they are to paper-based records. In their discussion of implementing an archival preservation program, Norvell Jones and Mary Lynn Ritzenthaler detail the interrelated factors that cause archival records to deteriorate: the chemical and physical stability of specific materials, storage under adverse environmental conditions, and external causes such as excessive or careless handling, and loss or destruction brought about by human-induced or natural disasters.[2] In every case the factors on this list are factors that must be considered in the preservation of electronic records as well. An understanding of the physical properties of electronic records and the environmental conditions that they should be stored under are essential for ensuring that the information stored on these records is preserved.

ELEMENTS OF A PRESERVATION PROGRAM

The seven elements of a preservation program: *environment, storage, handling and use, microreproduction and reformatting, exhibition, disaster planning,* and *treatment* must be considered by an institution charged with preserving electronic records. The only element that does not have real importance in electronic records is exhibition. One of the most important differences between textual records and electronic records is the inapplicability of the concept of original document with electronic media. Perhaps the closest approximation of the original document is the disk on which the information is first captured. But electronic media may be stored in a number of ways at any point in its evolution to the output that an archives or library receives. With electronic records, one is not concerned with the physical object, because the physical nature does not convey any information about the past and how the record was created. The physical object simply provides the medium on which to store the information.[3]

In the preservation literature, there appears to be greater emphasis placed on ensuring the permanence of the information in records rather than on the documents themselves. This change in emphasis may be in reaction to the greater prominence of electronic formats as a means of preservation and distribution of information. Ms. Kenney's discussion of the project at Cornell in which optical disk technology is being used to reformat the information currently found in books that are too fragile to use is one facet of this new direction.[4]

To reiterate, the seven elements of a preservation program, environment, storage, handling and use, microreproduction and reformatting, disaster planning and treatment, should be considered in any preservation plan that includes electronic records. Let me stress that, as in paper records, perhaps the most important area in dealing with electronic media is environment. Electronic records, like other audiovisual records, require temperatures between 62 and 68 degrees Fahrenheit, with an optimum temperature of 65 degrees. (George Cunha says that 66–70 degrees is a compromise for what is best for books in libraries and requirements for the comfort of staff and patrons.) The relative humidity requirements are different for audiovisual materials, particularly for magnetic tape versus paper. Humidity levels between 35 and 45 percent with an optimum of 40 (Geller) is the recommended level according to the National Institute of Standards and Technology (formerly the National Bureau of Standards). These levels are lower than the 50 percent recommended for paper records. According to George Cunha, the commonly accepted view at this time is that if audiovisual materials such as magnetic tape cannot be isolated in a mini-environment, then the overall humidity in the building should be kept between 40 and 50 percent. He emphasizes, "it is far more important to stabilize both temperature and humidity at points as near as possible to the optimum conditions than to strive for optimum conditions with heating and cooling machinery that is unequal to the task and likely to produce constantly fluctuating temperature and humidity levels."[5]

The proper storage and handling of archival materials can be the single most important aspect of a preservation program, particularly for paper records; but again, this is also applicable to electronic records.[6] Proper storage includes placing open reel tapes in plastic canisters and storing these tapes or cartridges vertically in shelving constructed specifically for open tape reels or tape cartridges. Unlike paper, which can be stored indefinitely if placed in the proper containers, reels should be exercised periodically (there is discussion as to how often this should be done), and there should be a periodic inspection of a random sample of files to test the readability of the media. An interesting theory proposed by Margaret Adams who oversees the reference activities at the Center for Electronic Records is that, unlike paper records, reference activity actively promotes preservation in electronic records because the staff uses the files thereby determining the readability of that specific file. The media is also cleaned and rewound after each use thus ensuring proper tensioning of the media.

Cinching, which occurs when portions of the tape move unevenly on the tape drive, and stretching can cause serious problems. Distortion of the data due to improper tension or shrinking or expansion of the tape, or erasure of the tape can lead to the loss of the information stored on the tape. Improper handling of magnetic tapes or tape cartridges can cause edge damage as well. Thus procedures for ensuring the proper handling of electronic media must be an integral part of a preservation program for electronic records.[7]

Reformatting, the next element in a preservation program, is absolutely essential when electronic records are concerned. This is the second great distinction between textual and electronic records. The first was the inapplicability of the concept of original document. The second difference is the requirement of moving electronic records to new formats to keep up with the ever-changing technology. As the National Research Council pointed out in their study "Preservation of Historical Records" and the National Institute of Standards and Technology (NIST) has confirmed, the recording media in use may well outlast the hardware, thus making it necessary to recopy the electronic file every 10 to 20 years to ensure access to the information. This recopying process simply reformats the information to avoid obsolescence. The information is not changed in any way.[8]

The National Archives has an established recopying program in place, making two new copies of every file every ten years. Since March of this year, all new copies are being created on tape cartridge. Most of the files that are ten years old are on 1600 bpi open reel tape. Both of these formats can be accessed with current tape drives, but within a few years it will be difficult to find computer centers that have tape drives that can read the 1600 bpi tapes. Hence, the move to tape cartridge, which is the de facto standard for most large tape libraries. It is also as reliable as older magnetic tape media, which is not true for other new media.

Disaster Planning

Disaster planning must be a part of any preservation program. Electronic records are susceptible to water and fire damage. The best way to protect the information in electronic format is by making a second copy of any file and storing it off-site. The National Archives creates two copies of every file that is transferred to the National Archives. The copy that is used for making reference copies is stored at the main building to provide easy access for any requests. A second copy, or master copy is stored off-site in case of any unforeseen disaster.

Treatment, the last element discussed by Jones and Ritzenthaler, does not figure as prominently with electronic records, although the National Archives recently encountered problems with some of its older tapes and is working with the National Media Lab in Minneapolis, Minnesota to find a way to salvage as much of the information from these tapes as possible. Generally, the best method of treatment is prevention, recopying electronic files before serious problems develop.

I have briefly described the basic elements of a general preservation program and detailed the similarities and differences between textual and electronic records in implementing a preservation program. Now I would like to focus more directly on the problems posed by electronic records for any institution seeking to preserve the information found on this media. The rest of the paper will be devoted to the problems of preserving electronic records. I must stress that there are two types of preservation for electronic media. The more easily recognizable is the physical preservation, which I will discuss next. There is a second type of preservation as well, intellectual preservation, which I will discuss briefly at the end of this paper.

Most people concerned with the preservation of any media focus on the physical preservation of that media. With electronic records there are two problems: the fragility of the medium and the obsolescence of the technology on which the information is stored. When I detailed the similarities and differences between electronic records and textual records, I described some of the steps necessary to ensure preservation of the electronic information. Because I touched on this topic only briefly, I want to correct any false impressions of easy solutions I might have made by stating emphatically that magnetic tape is a fragile medium. It should not be considered a form of permanent storage. Storage conditions and environment play crucial roles in determining how long the information will remain readable. As Bruce Ambacher summarizes in his article on "Managing Machine-Readable Archives" if this type of media is stored improperly, "...information encoded as magnetic or electronic impulses can become unreadable through deterioration of the physical surface, interference with the electronic signal, distortion of the data due to improper tension or shrinking or expansion of the tape, or erasure of the information...by writing over of the files by the computer center."[9] In cataloging the losses of valuable space science data at the National Aeronautics and Space Administration, the General Accounting Office specifically cited poor storage conditions as one of the crucial factors causing the deterioration of the stored electronic data.[10]

If magnetic tape is fragile, why then is it so widely used for storing electronic records? As the report issued by the House Committee on Government Operations, *Taking A Byte Out of History: The Archival Preservation of Federal Computer Records*, observes, "Magnetic computer tape has emerged over the past two decades as the prevalent mass storage medium used for both intermediate and archival data storage."[11] Magnetic tape has proven to be the most stable and least costly of the magnetic media available. Perhaps one of the most important factors has been the existence of well-established standards for open reel tape. Except for some exceptional cases where special tape drives have been developed for specific uses, almost any reel of commercially produced tape can be mounted on a tape drive, as long as it is at the specified density of that drive, and can be accessed by the computer system. This is equally true for the 3480 class tape cartridges. They have become the de facto standard for most computer centers.

Thus, we have a situation in which magnetic tape is used as the storage medium for electronic information, but it does not provide the permanence that most institutions would like to have for information they intend to maintain over a long period of time. One of the most widely accepted views about optical disk technology is its inherent stability, hence the view that this technology can provide a permanence not found in magnetic media. Unfortunately, while the medium may be extremely stable, possibly providing shelf lives of up to one hundred years, there remains the threat of the inability to read the information on this media because within ten years it will be difficult, if not impossible, to find drives capable of reading the disks created today.[12] The problem simply stated is the lack of standardization, making obsolescence of technology much more significant than with tape. While open reel tape drives can access almost any open reel tape, an optical disk can only be read by the system that created that disk. Hence, once a manufacturer moves from one system to another, there is an excellent chance that one will not be able to use the new system to gain access to the disk that was created on the older system. Unless the system has backwards compatibility, enabling a user to mount the older disks on the newer system, the information will have to be moved to the new system as quickly as possible or one will have to find ways of maintaining the outdated system for as long as possible.

Actually, one of the ways that the National Archives insures access to its files is by planned recopying of the files every ten years, moving to a newer technology if it is warranted. During this current year we have begun to copy to 3480 tape cartridges so the ten year recopying program is using the 3480 cartridges, moving from 1600 or 6250 bpi open reel tape to the 3480 tape cartridge. I am reluctant to predict what will be the recognized standard in ten years, but I am confident that the Center will be monitoring the developments in storage technology and will choose one that is recognized as a stable technology that will be around for at least ten years.

At this point, let me stress that I am not dismissing the utility of optical disks for various projects. Optical disk technology provides answers for a wide variety of situations, one of which I have just mentioned here. My position comes from the knowledge that the Center must be able to provide access to the information that has been transferred to the National Archives in electronic format for the foreseeable future. With the immense variety of file formats, hardware, and software used by Federal agencies, the Center has tried to define the most reasonable approach for transferring these files to the National Archives. Open reel or tape cartridge provides the most favorable means for the Center to make the copies that can then be made available for research. The lack of standardization in optical systems would make our difficult job totally impossible. But for institutions interested in providing information on optical systems, the issue of transferring to another media is not there. As long as your focus is not on long-term preservation, but rather immediate access to information that is being distributed to a wide audience, then optical systems are probably appropriate. If, on the other hand you are charged with the long term preservation of information in electronic format, you should look carefully at the problems posed by the lack of standardization in optical disk systems.

So, if magnetic media is fragile and nonpermanent and the technology to which it is directly attached has, in effect, planned obsolescence, why should any institution want to deal with this magnetic media? Why not just print out the information on the tape onto paper? There are two reasons: the ability to use the computer to manipulate the data in ways unforseen when the electronic file was originally created or use various files that share some related information to develop new analyses and conclusions, and perhaps even more importantly, because of the issues of space and money.

The current standard magnetic tape is half an inch wide and 2,400 feet long. The data is encoded on open reel tape at 6250 bytes or characters per inch. At this level of compaction a standard reel of tape can store up to 180 million characters or the equivalent of 50,000 to 75,000 pages of text. The same amount of information stored on paper would occupy up to 135 cubic feet of space.[13]

Let me provide a specific example of the difference in cost in storing information in electronic format as opposed to printing it out at the National Archives. The Director of the Center performed some cost analysis to determine what exactly the costs were in preserving electronic records. He included computer resources, supplies and salaries for verifying accessions, creating preservation copies, performing holdings maintenance, conducting annual samples, periodically copying all of the electronic files onto new media and all other activities relating to these functions. He found that all these activities translated into the Center spending less than $25 per reel per year. Storage costs at the National Archives building are estimated at less than $10 per cubic foot per year. Six reels of magnetic tape fit into a cubic foot, so the total cost per cubic foot was approximately $160.

I will grant you that this is a lot more than $10 for simple storage costs. However, if the electronic records stored in that one cubic foot are printed out and saved as paper, they would fill 360 cubic feet. That's almost $3600 for space alone, ignoring any costs for processing, holdings maintenance, or preservation.

Perhaps even more interesting is that the costs for preserving electronic files are decreasing. Whereas five years ago it was estimated that the costs for identifying, inventorying, scheduling, appraising, accessioning, and initial preservation were approximately $400 in both staff and computer hardware and accessory costs, current estimates place the costs for these same activities at approximately $300 per reel. At the present time, the Center for Electronic Records uses a computer center at the National Institutes of Health for processing electronic files that are transferred to the National Archives. In the past year, the costs for processing these files has decreased. In fiscal year 1990, the Center used the computer center to perform analysis on many of our files and copied 278 data files at an annual cost of $38,463 or $133.36 per file. The next year saw the Center copying 690 files at a cost of $51,340 or $74.40 per file. Beginning in October of 1991 through March 1992, the Center copied 508 files at a cost of $21,584, or $42.49 per file. Thus we are copying more files at less cost, which mirrors a trend that most of you have noticed. The cost of equipment has decreased as the machines have become more powerful, permitting greater efficiencies in performing the work assigned to that system. This trend will probably continue. The revolution of the microcomputer has not yet reached its final stages. So the viability of instituting a preservation program is promising, given the constant improvements in the technology arena.

However, let me provide a cautionary note. As all of you are aware, we live in a time of limited resources. When we agree to accept custody of records, we also accept responsibility for insuring their preservation. However, no institution has the ability to accept every collection that it is offered. As Margaret Child elucidates in her article on microfilming, there must be an awareness that "the traditional archival commitment to preserve entails potentially large expenditures of effort and money..." and this awareness should underlie every decision to acquire, appraise, house and make available these records for research use.[14] Thus, if your institution decides to preserve electronic records, it should base its decision on the awareness of the likely costs that will be entailed by accepting these files.

A key function performed by the technical staff at the Center for Electronic Records is the technical analysis of the electronic files that are being considered for transfer. Technical considerations can be equal to or even override decisions as to the long-term value of the information contained in the file. The technical factors cannot be overlooked: these include the readability of the records, the adequacy of the documentation associated with the file, the hardware and software considerations, and of greatest interest to this group, the preservation requirements.[15] Thus, preservation considerations must be included in the appraisal which leads to the decision whether to accept or reject the files being offered for transfer. The costs that will be incurred in accepting these files must be considered by an institution. To accept files that will not be properly preserved is a disservice to the user community.

Preserving electronic records means preserving the ability to process these records on a computer. The Center for Electronic Records has a program to assure this requirement, by insuring proper environmental conditions and proper storage and handling to prevent degradation of the data, and by providing transportability of the data with the systematic copying of the files onto a format that will remain accessible for at least ten years.

When an electronic file has been transferred to the National Archives, the Technical Services Branch and the Archival Services Branch work together to determine if the agency sent the correct tape; if the Center can process the tape on the computer that we use at the National Institutes of Health; if the tape is readable, that is, there are no datachecks on the tape; and if the agency included the necessary documentation when it sent the file to the National Archives. After all of these initial questions have been answered in the affirmative, the Technical Services Branch makes two archival copies of the file onto 3480 cartridges which have been evaluated and certified for copying. The reference copy, which is stored at the National Archives building, is used for filling orders when researchers decide that they want a copy of the file. The master copy is stored off-site and is only used when the Center discovers a problem with the reference copy.

The staff monitors the environmental conditions, preparing a quarterly report of the temperature and humidity ranges as reported on the hygrothermagraphs that are placed in the storage vaults. The Center also invited the National Media Lab to conduct atmospheric tests of some of our vaults. Based on their findings we have instituted a program for cleaning all of our canisters that are stored off-site to avoid the possibility of contamination by mold spores, which the National Media Lab found at that site.

All reels are stored in canisters, vertically in tape racks. If a reel is placed on a tape drive for any reason, for reference copying, as part of the annual sample, or for testing purposes, the tape is cleaned and rewound to remove any debris transferred from the tape drive to the tape reel and to ensure a controlled rewind to prevent edge damage and tape folding or cinching.

The Center selects a sample of its holdings each year and verifies that the file is readable. If we encounter datachecks on the files tested, they are immediately recopied. We are currently performing our annual sample, testing the readability of 384 data files in our custody.

To insure transportability we have a program for recopying the data files every ten years. During this fiscal year we plan to copy 276 files that are ten years old.

To summarize, the Center for Electronic Records has the responsibility for making the preservation copies, monitoring the vault conditions, and performing the other maintenance to ensure the preservation of the data stored on these magnetic tapes and tape cartridges. These activities require major expenditure both in human and financial resources. Currently there are sixteen full-time staff and six part-time staff to perform this work. The positions include archivists, computer analysts, computer programmers and archives technicians. Personnel costs are approximately $500,000 and my budget includes $75,000 for computer processing costs at the National Institutes of Health.

Although my paper has emphasized the physical preservation of electronic files, there is also the intellectual preservation that must be considered. Unlike textual records, electronic files require documentation for comprehending the information found in these data files. Appropriate documentation must be available to provide the necessary information on the digital codes used, the organization or format of the file, and the explanation of how and why the file was created. Without proper documentation the file is inaccessible and the information lost. If, in appraising a data file that is being considered for transfer to the National Archives, the appraisal archivist discovers that the documentation no longer exists, this alone justifies the decision not to accept the file for transfer.

A second aspect of intellectual preservation, particularly with newer forms of electronic records concerns relational databases, that is, the capture of the relationships between the various tables that store the information in the databases. The National Archives has an application developed by the ORACLE Corporation to assist us in capturing the relationships found in databases. The Archival Electronic Records Inspection and Control system is being developed both to provide automated validation of newly transferred electronic files and to enable the National Archives to capture and preserve the structure even of very complex databases through the specification, in Standard Query Language (SQL), of the relationships between and among files in the database. SQL is a standard database management tool. The National Archives can use SQL to preserve database structures independently of the software which had been used to express these formats in the originating agency. We intend to use this system to begin processing some of the Census files that are being transferred to us. As the Center gains experience with this application, we will extend it to capture the structures of databases that are offered to us.

I have appreciated the opportunity of discussing the issues pertaining to the preservation of electronic records. My hope is that by providing a framework and then specific examples of how preservation is accomplished in electronic records, that you will have a better understanding of the elements of an electronic preservation program, so that those who are interested in inaugurating such a program can begin to plan how this can be implemented.

Notes

1. Anne R. Kenney, "From the Editor," *American Archivist*, vol. 53, no. 2, Spring 1990, 184.

2. Norvell M. M. Jones and Mary Lynn Ritzenthaler, "Implementing an Archival Preservation Program," in *Managing Archives and Archival Institutions*, ed. James Gregory Bradsher (Chicago: The University of Chicago Press, 1988), 188.

3. Ibid, 188–196.

4. Janet E. Gertz, "Preservation Microfilming for Archives and Manuscripts," *The American Archivist*, vol. 53, no. 2, Spring 1990, 228.

5. George Martin Cunha, "Current Trends in Preservation Research and Development," *The American Archivist*, vol. 53, no.2, Spring 1990, 195. Sidney B. Geller, *Care and Handling of Computer Magnetic Storage Media*, National Bureau of Standards Special Publication 500–101, (Washington, D.C: National Bureau of Standards, 1983), 86.

6. Jones and Ritzenthaler, 191–2.

7. Bruse I. Ambacher, "Managing Machine-Readable Archives," *Managing Archives and Archival Institutions*, ed. James Gregory Bradsher (Chicago: University of Chicago Press, 1988), 124–5.

8. National Research Council, *Preservation of Historical Records*, (Washington D.C.: National Academy Press, 1986), 61–2.

9. Ambacher, "Managing Machine-Readable Archives," 124–5.

10. General Accounting Office, "Space Operations: NASA Is Not Properly Safeguarding Valuable Data From Past Missions," (1990) (GAO/IMTEC-90–1).

11. Congress, House Committee on Government Operations, *Taking a Byte Out of History: The Archival Preservation of Federal Computer Records*, 101st Cong., 2d sess., 1990, H.R., 29.

12. Kenneth Thibodeau, "The Preservation of Electronic Records: Keynote Address," National Archives and Records Administration Annual Preservation Conference, Washington, D.C.: March 19, 1991, 9.

13. Ambacher, 124.

14. Margaret S. Child, "Selection for Microfilming," *The American Archivist*, vol. 53, no. 2, Spring 1990, 255.

15. Ambacher, 129.

Bibliography

"The Archives of the Future: Archival Strategies for the Treatment of Electronic Databases." *A Report for the National Archives and Records Administration*, revised December 1991.

Ambacher, Bruce I. "Managing Machine-Readable Archives," in *Managing Archives and Archival Information*, ed. James Gregory Bradsher, pp. 121–133. Chicago: University of Chicago Press, 1988.

Child, Margaret S. "Selection for Microfilming," *The American Archivist*, 53 (Spring 1990): 250–255.

Conway, Paul. "Archival Preservation Practice in a Nationwide Context," *The American Archivist*, 53 (Spring 1990): 204–222.

Cunha, George Martin. "Current Trends in Preservation Research and Development," *The American Archivist* 53 (Spring 1990): 192–202.

Eaton, Fynette L. "Current Practices in the Preservation of Electronic Records at the National Archives." National Archives and Records Administration Annual Preservation Conference, Washington, D.C., March 19, 1991.

Geller, Sidney B. *Care and Handling of Computer Magnetic Storage Media.* National Bureau of Standards Special Publication 500–101. Washington, D.C.: National Bureau of Standards, 1983.

Gertz, Janet E. "Preservation Microfilming for Archives and Manuscripts," *The American Archivist* 53 (Spring 1990): 224–234.

Hedstrom, Margaret L. *Archives and Manuscripts: Machine-Readable Records.* Chicago: Society of American Archivists, 1984.

Jones, Norvell M.M. and Ritzenthaler, Mary Lynn. "Implementing an Archival Preservation Program," in *Managing Archives and Archival Information*, ed. Janes Gregory Bradsher, pp. 185–206. Chicago: University of Chicago Press, 1988.

National Archives and Records Administration. *Managing Electronic Records.* National Archives and Records Administration Instructional Guide Series. Washington, D.C.: National Archives, 1990.

National Archives and Records Administration. "Strategy for Electronic Records." NARA Response to OMB. Washington, D.C.: National Archives, July 1991.

"A National Archives Strategy for the Development and Implementation of Standards for the Creation, Transfer, Access and Long-Term Storage of Electronic Records of the Federal Government." National Archives

Technical Information Paper No. 8. Archival Research and Evaluation Staff. National Archives, Washington, D.C., June 1990.

National Research Council. *Preservation of Historical Records.* Washington, D.C.: National Academy Press, 1986.

Thibodeau, Kenneth. "The Preservation of Electronic Records: Keynote Address." National Archives and Records Administration Annual Preservation Conference, Washington, D.C., March 19, 1991.

U.S. Congress. House of Representatives. Committee on Government Operations, *Taking a Byte Out of History: The Archival Preservation of Federal Computer Records.* 101st Congress, 2nd Session, 1990. H.R.987.

Weir, Thomas E., Jr. "3480 Class Tape Cartridge Drives and Archival Data Storage: Technology Assessment Report," Technical Information Paper No. 4, Archival Research and Evaluation Staff. National Archives, Washington, D.C., June 1988.

Williamson, Mark P. *The 3480 Type Tape Cartridge: Potential Data Storage Risks, and Care and Handling Procedures to Minimize Risks.* National Institute of Standards and Technology Special Publication 500–199. Washington, D.C.: National Institute of Standards and Technology, 1991.

Discussion

Q. Did you study the effects of mold on optical disks?

A. No, we have not looked at the issue, because we do not preserve information on that type of media. We discovered the possibility of mold in our off-site storage location, which we share with the other units of the National Archives, when the National Media Lab was analyzing the environmental conditions of our storage areas. Their chemical analyses indicated the existence of mold spores and the additional conditions of high humidity and little or no air movement in that area meant that we might have a problem with mold. I was very concerned, because if our tapes were contaminated, they could contaminate the tape drives at the computer center we use at the National Institutes of Health. When we asked the National Media Lab for their recommendation, they indicated that there probably was no need for concern because the tapes are stored in canisters and they are also enclosed in plastic. They suggested that we remove the plastic bags and wipe off the canisters when we send the tapes to the computer center, which we now do. So we were concerned with magnetic tape and the mold spores, not optical media. Do I think mold effects optical disks? I am not sure, since I am not an expert on optical technology. I think that it would be a good question to ask the people who have come to talk about CD-ROM. My experience is with magnetic tape.

Q. *Two questions: one, the SQL software that will allow you to access data independent of the original software, does it also allow you to manipulate the data in the same way that the original software did?*

A. First, SQL is like any other relational database. Second, you should be able to access data independent of the original software, as long as the file is in a format that you can access on your computer. We will not use SQL for that purpose at present because we have a specific need to capture the relationships in relational files to enable us to document how the files were created. However, that does not preclude us from using it for other purposes at a later point. We are proposing to increase the level of reference service when we move to our new building at College Park, Maryland, in 1994. We plan to build a front end to the AERIC system to enable researchers to take information from different files and combine this information, using SQL. So we will make this type of inquiry available to researchers.

Q. *My other question is, Taking a Bite Out of History is a really overwhelming report in terms of the difficulty it points up, in trying to hold onto computer files. And one of the themes that seemed to emerge from that report was the problem of standards being developed very slowly. The cutting edge technology, true cutting edge technology creates lots and lots of non-standard files while the standard setting is way back in the past. The report points up the difficulty of our moving ahead very fast without mechanisms for holding on to everything we're creating at this time, protocols for hardware, software, documentation and so forth. Is there, how has NARA responded to that report?*

A. May I do this as my opinion? You are correct in that we have a serious problem in the proliferation of new technologies. In responding to *Taking a Byte,* the National Archives stressed that it was attempting to address these issues systemically in small steps. I'm with the office that has custodial responsibilities for Federal electronic records. A second office, the Archival Research and Evaluation Staff, currently have staff participating on the standards boards. NARA is trying to get involved in the standards process, but it is extremely slow. I think *Taking a Byte* was taking us to task because we are not doing everything at one time. Part of the problem is that we receive files when agencies transfer them to us. What we are receiving now, in most cases, are the older files, because agencies apply the procedures they use for paper records, of transferring paper files after 30 years, to computer files as well. I am concerned that the information will be lost if agencies wait for 30 years.

We are now trying to convince agencies to transfer their electronic files as soon as possible. NARA is using the NAPA study to provide entry to agencies, asking them to transfer files to us immediately. Until recently, we have been receiving only the older files, created in the 1970s and early 1980s that are hardware- and software-independent, which we are accustomed to handling. With newer, more complex files we hope to use AERIC to deal with software-dependent files and with relational databases.

NARA is also examining issues surrounding some of the newer technologies. One staff member is looking at CD-ROMs. Will the National Archives use CD-ROMs as a distribution medium or should we consider it as a possible storage medium? Another staff member is looking at the issues posed by Geographic Information Systems. What types of files are being create by agencies? How will these new types of files impact what we are doing at the National Archives? So, we do not have immediate answers to many of the questions posed by *Taking a Byte*, but I think we can use the report as a base to develop some specific programs that begin to address the issues found in that publication. In many ways I viewed the report as an opportunity, because it brought the issues forward to a larger audience. In this way, I view it as a positive document.

Q. At what point will the National Archives switch from using magnetic tape to some other medium?

A. The National Archives monitors the use of storage media. We must use a media that is widely used and is standardized. We will not use optical disks, at least at this point, because there are no standards for hardware and software associated with optical systems. We cannot invest in an optical system, only to convert to another media with the obsolescence of that equipment. We've used magnetic tape for 20 years. It's not perfect, but it has worked well. We have not lost data, so we will continue to use it until we can find something better. New products are constantly being produced, but we will work with people from the Archival Research and Evaluation Staff at NARA, the National Institute of Standards and Technology, and the National Media Lab to monitor these developments.

Q. *Our concern is, the physical properties of the item are important to researchers. Is there a way to combine the properties of the magnetic tape and image capture so that you could have on the leader of the tape a picture of the physical item, or is that a stupid question?*

A. No, the issue of physical property for magnetic tape does not have the same relevance as for other media. Like sound recordings, it is the information contained on the media that is important, not the outside container. If you copy a sound recording, would you hold onto the original sound recording to show what it was originally recorded on?

Q. *From many perspectives the jacket is very valuable....*

A. A magnetic tape is stored in a canister. Normally the only information on the canister is a volume serial number. If there is any additional information on the canister that is recorded and put in the documentation that accompanies the electronic file. The tape itself is simply a medium of storage.

Q. *Getting back to the reference services available at the National Archives, I know you said you didn't provide a lot of service, but what software is available to researchers?*

A. At the Center for Electronic Records we provide copies of the basic data. We assume that the researcher will use software that they have access to for processing the file that we have sent them. We do not normally provide software for analyzing the files. There is one exception. One agency has transferred the files both as raw data and in SPSS format as well. We will keep both versions of the file until we recopy the file in ten years. At that point, we will only copy the raw data, because the SPSS software will have undergone so many changes that the file will be inaccessible, probably after five years. If standards evolve for software, then we might consider it. For example, most Federal offices use WordPerfect. Perhaps it will evolve into the one word processing software used by all government agencies. Then we would consider accepting files in WordPerfect. Geographical Information Systems pose problems because they are software dependent. That is one of the issues we are studying with GIS.

Q. As a general rule, what determines if the Archives will accept particular software?

A. If an agency offers software, we will ask the question, "Does the software provide unique documentation on how specific decisions or actions came about?" What we are interested in is documenting government activity.

Q. Oftentimes on a government report you have a coversheet where department heads will sign off on it. How much of that information goes into your database? And how is that presented? For example, where somebody signs it, and how they sign it can be important.

A. OK, you are basically asking about text files that capture the different levels of review electronically. We have not received those types of files from agencies yet. Our holdings consist of Census files, statistical files, surveys, etc. Electronic mail is of real interest to us: we intend to look at this issue, but we have not yet had any experience with this type of record. We are working with the Supreme Court to transfer the final rulings by the Court in electronic format to gain experience in text files.

Q. If you have a Census file, where on your magnetic tape can you show, how do you show that the information is accurate?

A. When an agency transfers an electronic file they sign a form which states that they are transferring a complete and accurate file to the National Archives. So we assume that the information is complete. I want to emphasize that when we receive a file, we do not make any corrections; we do not touch the data. If the person who created the file made a mistake, we retain that mistake, because that's how they've made their decisions. When we copy the file to our own tapes, we run a program which performs a byte to byte comparison, which provides the necessary proof that it is an exact copy of the information on the agency tape.

Q. How do your researchers find out about your tapes and then get access to them?

A. The Center has created a Title List which provides information about the files that are available to researchers. We also monitor the Archives ListServe and answer specific inquiries about our holdings. To gain access to our holdings, one can write and ask specific questions, or one can visit and look at the documentation related to the files. However, if you want to look at the file, you must order a copy of it. This is why I have said we do not perform extensive reference service: we make copies of files, but cannot provide direct access to the information. As I stated in my presentation, currently we do not have our own computer, so if someone wants a file, all that we are able to do at this point is to make a copy of that file. Currently we do not produce extracts or printouts. It is our hope that when we move to Archives II we will be able to increase the types of reference service on electronic records.

Q. A follow-up to an earlier question, the documentation that you look for before you decide to accession a record on, do you insist on this certification that the electronic file is what it is?

A. When an agency transfers an electronic file and the documentation that relates to this file, they sign a form which in effect states this is the file that should be transferred. It is this form that in effect certifies to us that it is the complete file that is being transferred.

Q. Then you keep a paper trail to go along with it?

A. We have documentation that accompanies the electronic file, which explains the codes and how the file was created. For anyone to be able to use a file, there must be explanations of the codes and layout of the file. In many cases this is on paper. However, a lot of agencies are moving to putting that documentation in electronic format as well.

Q. When the Center does accession, do you know if that is at all coupled with the disposal of the paper records or the electronic records of the agency?

A. The National Archives has an office responsible for the scheduling and appraisal of Federal records. The Center has the responsibility of appraising electronic files, so when both paper and electronic records are being considered, there is coordination between the two offices. The agency proposes a schedule for all of its records, which includes recommendations for disposal, be it transfer to the National Archives or destruction of the files after a certain time period. If there is an electronic file, the Center receives the schedule and works with the agency to determine if the file should be transferred to the National Archives. One of the critical issues is if the agency has the documentation associated with the file. While we are looking at the electronic records, the Office of Administration is looking at the paper records. In many cases, the Center will consider an automated index to correspondence files. In this situation the Archives will bring in both the paper file and the automated index. Does that answer your question?

Q. Yes. I was just wondering if there is a coupling or connection, the implication being that records are being disposed of as they are accessioned, that agency files are being disposed of at the same time that you accession them at the Center....

A. Are you talking about electronic records and how they're disposed of? Electronic records provide an unique opportunity for the National Archives, because we are able to tell an agency, send us a copy of the file; an agency does not have to send us the original copy—because there is no such thing as a unique copy of electronic information. And after we have completed making two copies of the file, we return the tape back to the agency. Thus, the agency is not losing the tape and if they transfer the file to us, we accept the responsibility for preserving the information. The agency no longer has to worry about preserving the file—the National Archives has it. It is the National Archives responsibility, its mission is to preserve that information. That is why we exist. An agency many times will want to continue to use the information, which is fine, as long as the information has been transferred to us in an acceptable format. We are working very closely with the Census Bureau. They are sending us the summary tape files for the 1990 Census. This program comes out of the problems with the 1960 and 1970 files, Census has had to spend hundreds of thousands of dollars to convert files to a format that the Archives can accept. By transferring the 1990 Census now, they avoid the costly problems of the older files, and they no longer have to worry about preserving these files, since they are now part of our holdings.

Q. Back to mold briefly, can you tell me if there are any references I can look at for the susceptibility of this medium to mold?

A. At this point, no.

About the Author

Fynette Eaton has a B.A. and a M.A. in British History from the University of Maryland. She has worked at two archival institutions, The Archives of American Art, 1976–77, and the National Archives and Records Administration, 1977–present. As an archivist, Ms. Eaton worked in the Office of Presidential Libraries, with the audiovisual materials from various Presidential libraries. She also worked with the Documentation Standards Staff and in 1986 she joined the Machine-Readable Branch. She has been with this office, which is now the Center for Electronic Records, concentrating on the preservation activities of electronic records. She is currently Branch Chief of the Technical Services Branch.

4

The Electronic Document Image Preservation Format

Basil Manns
Physical Scientist
Library of Congress

INTRODUCTION

When applied to the preservation and access of electronic documents or images, the phrase "electronic formats" means different things to different people. Format by itself is a confusing term. In the library preservation community it often refers to the physical media as format: paper, book, or a variety of microform. Data processors refer to format as the logical order of data and control information stored in a machine. System integrators map the logical format structure of the data on a specific medium that the machine accesses. In order for things to work the way we want them to, we all need to understand a little about all of this.

This paper discusses format issues for the preservation and access of electronic documents. In doing so, both the logical formats and the media formats need to be discussed and understood. Formatting implies how the document is captured, processed, and stored for future access. Issues such as efficiencies, perception, reliability, lossness, interoperability, longevity, and certification are all involved. Everyone need not understand how all the processing really works, but everyone does need to know how to make it work correctly.

No question should exist in anyone's mind regarding the need for and importance of electronic document preservation, both for publications originally formatted on electronic media and for source documents that have been converted to electronic media. A recent study commissioned by AIIM and performed by Deloitte & Touche, looked at the state of the information and image management (I&IM) industry as of 1991. The study states that the I&IM industry growth rate from 1991 to 1995 (compounded annually) will be 28%. This estimate is conservative.

The Library of Congress is interested in moving the Library from being a passive repository for a scholarly and political elite into an active catalyst for revitalized information. This cannot happen without the electronic conversion of and access to the vast collection in the Library.

THE IMAGE FORMAT

The image format defines how the image is captured and recorded onto the medium of choice for further access. Document management predominately uses raster imaging to represent the captured image, be it from a book, magazine, or some other artifact. In the raster mode, the image is a collection of picture elements. These picture elements, called pixels or pels, make up the electronic image. Pixels are analogous to the tesserae with which a mosaic is composed. Pixels are located in a grid array in which each pixel has its own location and only one value of brightness or color. These pixels make up the digital image. Each pixel is small and from a distance the digital image can be made to appear "quite good" for a particular application.

The raster image is, then, an orderly array of pixels swept across a CRT for display, or projected onto a laser drum for printing. In both cases the image is synchronized with the orientation of the output device. In the printing industry, the term dots is used, rather than pixels.

The raster image contains no information. It is just a collection of pixels, each having no meaning. Raster images need to be differentiated from graphic images. Raster images are captured images and graphic images are created images. For example, a scanner captures an existing image into a computer. A set of commands given to the computer draws a graph or lines, fills an area, shades a space, or represents certain objects for the purpose of creating an artificial image. The term "synthetic image" is also used to mean computer-generated, artificial, or graphic images.

The raster image is non-coded data. Digital audio is also non-coded information, where each byte represents a level, like in brightness in a raster image, and by itself has no meaning. Text, on the other hand, is coded information. Each byte represents a word, a character, or has some meaning. Typically, text is encoded using ASCII language. Graphic images are also coded images, and for them each unit of information is a graphic command.

UNDERSTANDING THE DOCUMENT

There are numerous format types, using this term loosely, for defining digital images. Some have developed from national or international standards and some require user definitions, but most have developed from the manufacturers' need to integrate systems for particular applications. (See figure 1.) Some are layered and some can stand alone. Commonly used formats include CCITT Group III & Group IV, TIFF (Tagged Input File Format from Aldus, HPGL (Hewlett Package Graphic Language), PostScript, IOCA (Image Object Content Architecture from IBM), DIFF (DEC Image File Format), WIFF (Wang Image File Format), and SGML (Standard Generalized Markup Language). The list goes on, with many

---

Document Standards
Defined by ISO 8613 (ODA/ODIF)

- Test Standards: Well defined and used in many applications in documents
- Graphic Standards: Not as well defined, but of less interest in document image applications
- Raster Standards:
    Continuous Tone — JPEG
    Bi-Tonal — CCITT, JBIG

Figure 1: The Document Image

proprietary vendor formats. In any case, the object is to convert the physical page description of a document into a form that a machine can understand and process using certain pre-defined rules. This leads to the concept of "Document Understanding" and to the process of developing a document taxonomy for both physical and electronic documents.

We are all aware of the physical document. The taxonomy can be explained by looking at the page as a constructed object, and by defining the structure using defined attributes. Page or document understanding involves the breakdown of an object into physical attributes such as: bound vs. unbound, mass-printed vs. hand-printed, size, paper type, processed ink vs. photo-processed, reproduction vs. original, continuous tone, black and white photo, black and white body text, monochromatic body text, line art, halftones styles (inks, points, dots, and screen pitch and angle), and color. A true taxonomy will develop a tree, but in this case forms a list of observable descriptors. (See figure 2.).

```
• Bound or Unbound
• Mass Printed or Hand Printed
• Size
• Type of Paper
• Ink Type
• Reproduction or Original
• Continuous Tone, Color, B&W, or Halftone
• Line Art or Text
• Screen Pitch and Angle
• Layout of Objects on Page
```

Figure 2: Physical Page Taxonomy

There are physical document types such as newspapers, weeklies, journals, newsletters, program announcements, and so on. There are also format types such as manuscripts, monographs, serials, maps, musical materials, film, photographs, posters, audiotapes and recordings, and microforms. And third, there are the semantic content types such as a dictionary (granular) or novel (unitary). Another way of breaking down semantic content type is reference vs. literature. Finally, the interior of the item is broken down into its structure such as chapters, sections, paragraphs, lines, sentences, words, and other user defined structured descriptors

The electronic document taxonomy is viewed by information type such as coded vs. non-coded. Coded is constructed data such as text and graphic data as described earlier. Attributes of these data are artificial, generated, small, and intelligent. Non-coded is captured data, such as a raster image. It is real, observed, large, and not intelligent. It can be image or audio.

Examples of coded data used in document formats are ODA, SGML, word processor codes, Initial Graphics Exchange Specification (IGES), and Hewlett Packard Graphic Language (HPGL) to name a few. Some of these can even overlap because they are not only the format structure, but also facilitate the interchange of the documents.

Coded data are structured and are designed for processing a given application. In a page or document layout scheme, the structure would be defined as a tree starting, for example, from the report itself, then proceeding to the report heading, table of contents, chapters, chapter headings, sections, paragraphs, figures, pictures, caption, sentences, and so forth. These are well illustrated in ODA publications. Coded data, being intelligent, lend themselves to numerous schemes of indexing, which is another very important subject, but not to be discussed here.

As noted previously, non-coded data are captured, real, observed, and contain no intelligence. They are usually associated with raster data, but may also include digital audio. (Let's ignore the analog world of audio and video for now.) Their content types, associated with the necessary processing tools to capture and the necessary operations to display the image on a presentation medium, include: bi-level text, bi-level line art, bi-level halftone, gray scale (continuous tone), color halftone, and continuous tone color. Content attributes then would include: resolution, bits per pixel, color sampling, clipping position and size, orientation, and color space. Numerous color spaces are used, including RGB, YCrCb, CMYK, YUV, HSI, and indexed. Different applications favor different color spaces.

Many applications involve complex documents in which a page consists of various types of encoding schemes or a mixture of contents. A page could have text, image, and graphic illustrations. Numerous ways exist for capturing this page, and the term "compound document architecture" is used to define the process.

COMPRESSION

Image files are generally large in terms of the number of bits or bytes they require, and their creation usually involves some form of compression. The primary purpose of compression is to improve system performance and increase efficiencies. For example, compression reduces storage space, speeds up access time, and improves transmission time. Compression often involves more than just compression. It may also include some image processing to facilitate user applications. Aspects of the image may be cleaned up, deleted, improved, emphasized, or de-emphasized, depending upon the requirements of the user.

Images may also be scaled to match resolution, aspect ratio, or display features of the output devices (printers or monitors). For example, an 8 by 10 inch image scanned at 400 dpi will have 12.8 million pixels. This image, displayed on a 1024 by 768 super VGA screen, or 786 thousand pixels, reduces the number of pixels by a factor of more than 16. This is not compression. It is scaling. Scaling is often inadvertently and incorrectly combined with the data reduction of compression in expressing the overall effect of the compression algorithm. This mistake, of course, makes the compression look better than it actually is.

Compression is extremely important and very complex. Currently image compression activities in the industry are very active, driven by multi-media interests and other digital imaging applications. Compression schemes are becoming more complex and more efficient. More options are available to the user for meeting particular applications. These compression modes can be grouped by data types. The graphic and text are considered coded data and enjoy less complex compression schemes than the raster data (non-coded data files) used in most imaging systems.

Images can be grouped into two general categories: bi-level and continuous tone. Bi-level images are one color (usually black and white) text, writing, line art, digital halftone, or anything represented with pixel information of one bit in depth. Continuous tone images can be monochromatic, color, gray scale, or anything represented with pixel information of more than one bit in depth. Common pixel depth for document imaging systems is 4, 6, 8, or 16 bits, but can go as high as 24 or 32 bits for medical or special applications.

Most compression schemes used in the image processing of bi-level images use the CCITT (International Telegraph and Telephone Consultative Committee) standard. This is often referred to as Group III or Group IV corresponding to the T.4 and T.6 compression algorithm of the CCITT standard for FAX compression. The standard was developed for telecommunication applications, and optimized for compressing printed text. It uses what is known as the Huffman encoding schemes, which are based on predefined run lengths. It is used extensively for binary image compression (text, line art, or halftone) for lack of a better method.

Continuous tone images (gray scale or color) are not efficiently processed by the CCITT compression schemes. JPEG (Joint Photographic Experts Group), a joint ISO and CCITT committee, has developed an ISO standard defining the functionality of the process of compressing and decompressing continuous tone gray scale or color still images. The purpose was to have a scheme with the widest possible range of applications. This JPEG standard, known as JPEG, is currently being implemented in both software and hardware at what is called the "baseline option." Numerous options beyond the baseline are defined in this standard in order for it to meet the wide range of applications.

Standardizing the compression of continuous tone gray scale and color still images is of significant importance to the document image processing field. JPEG deals with these images in a way that will meet almost all user needs. It has almost unlimited options, which means that it is challenging for users to understand and optimize its use.

JPEG can be categorized into two broad processes: lossy and lossless. The baseline lossy scheme uses what is known as the Discrete Cosine Transform (DCT) with sequential representation. The sampling scheme converts the image to the frequency components using the DCT. By defining quantization coefficients, one can selectively eliminate information that does not contribute to the visual perception of the image. Thus, high compression ratios can be attained with very little visual image quality loss and the compression ratio can be selected based on the users desired image quality.

Two important concepts in JPEG are the lossy or lossless option, and the progressive or sequential option. (See figure 3.) These options must be specified when the image is compressed. Lossy (using DCT) can achieve very high compression ratios, from 50:1 to 100:1, or more. Lossy is useful in delivering an image to a user who does not need high resolution or high quality, i.e., all the details of the image. However, once an image is compressed in a given mode, it must be decompressed in the same mode. The advantage is that it permits a choice of image quality. There is a trade-off between compressed size of the image and the image quality, determined at the time of compression.

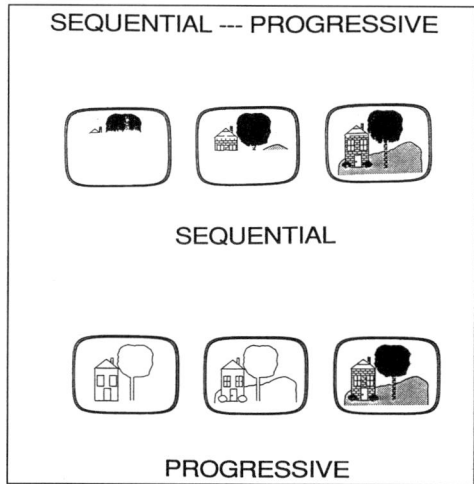

Figure 3: JPEG Options

The lossy compression scheme in JPEG also provides for the option of using a sequential or progressive mode. The sequential mode decompresses the compressed image in sequence from top to bottom, or from one end to the other. As a result, as the image is decompressed it is displayed on the screen sequentially, at its full information content. The progressive mode decompresses and displays the image relative to the quantization tables. The effect is to see the image "build up" on the screen, i.e., the outlines appear first, followed by more detail. The progressive mode has some advantages in that the complete image does not have to be decompressed before the user views the image, particularly if the user is in a browsing mode.

Lossless compression is also provided with JPEG but uses a different scheme, ADPCM (Adaptive Discrete Pulse Code Modulation). ADPCM is a predictive methodology in which successive pixels of an image are predicted based on the information obtained from its neighbors. No information is lost, but the compression ratio is considerably less than that of the DCT, typically 3:1 to 4:1. Since no information is lost, the visual image quality is maintained. ADPCM is suited for continuous tone gray scale or color images.

SELECTING A FORMAT

In selecting the appropriate format for a document, the first step is to go back to the taxonomy of the document. A large number of documents are basic page size and bi-tonal which leaves the user with few choices in selecting a methodology. Only the CCITT Group III or Group IV methodologies would be appropriate. Deciding on the resolution, pixel size, enhancement schemes, scan orientation, image size, and other minor attributes is straight forward. However, if the image is complex, i.e., coded data mixed with non-coded data, more attributes need to be considered. A structured approach using these attributes must be defined following the ODA format. AIIM (Association for Information and Image Management) is in the process of defining such a structure. The completion of this work will finally permit a raster image to be defined in compliance with the ODA standard.

For continuous tone or color images the format is more complex, but by using the JPEG compression scheme the attributes can be reduced to a manageable size. JPEG requires the Y, Cr, Cb color space as a document input. Three planes—8 bits, 4 bits, and 4 bits—correspond to the Y, Cr, and Cb color space, respectively. For gray scale images, only the Y plane is used. Scanning is usually done in the RGB or YCrCb color spaces. Displays are usually in the RGB or YUV color spaces. Processing is easiest in the HSI color space. Printing is best in the CMYK color space. Color space conversion programs are straight forward in theory, but actual color delivered to the user at a terminal or printer can vary considerably from the true color of the original. (See figure 4.)

Coded Data	**Non Coded Data**
Text	Raster
Graphics	

Figure 4: Document Image Taxonomy

WHAT USERS NEED TO DO

In using continuous tone or color systems for document conversion, three simple attributes must be defined. These are: 1) the resolution for scanning the document, 2) the levels of color or gray (maybe even binary), and 3) a lossy level.

The application should be the driving force in making these decisions. In this context, user needs are preservation and access. For preservation the highest resolution, the maximum number of levels for gray or color, and a lossless (or minimum lossyness) compression scheme are needed. These attributes can easily be achieved with JPEG, but testing of options for specific source materials must be done. General guidelines would not be adequate because original source materials vary so much. Very specific procedures must be defined based on image content and quality of output display.

For access, two types of formats may be used, depending on whether the access is for document delivery or for user browsing. The delivery copy must be of the highest or best image quality and, in all practical perceivable qualities, lossless. The browse copy can be of some "lower" image quality and lossy, in terms of the JPEG processes.

The access copies are produced from the preservation copy. Therefore, the preservation copy must be stored in a non-proprietary form that can be processed using standard schemes to produce anything from the best possible copy for delivery to a reduced-image-quality copy for browsing. High efficiency for a preservation copy is not essential.

Tools to determine the format needed to define a preservation file or the header for a preservation file include basic high-end scanning, processing, and output devices. The JPEG gray scale and color compression standard incorporates a great amount of flexibility but requires many decisions. These decisions need to be evaluated with regard to the preservation and access mission of the source documents. Evaluation needs to be done for the wide variety of source documents. A decision matrix for source documents and JPEG options needs to be developed and tested using a jury approach. Image quality is based on perception, and with a wide range of source documents we do not yet know what some of the results will be.

Testing would involve sampling categories of the collection (posters, maps, manuscripts, and so forth), providing both deliverable and browse copies to users, and tabulating user reaction to a wide range of compression and decompression schemes and display options. A test platform, configured with user selectable options and a wide range of scanning and output features, is essential. The test platform must be capable of selecting quantization coefficients and of judging the results on a variety of output devices.

The criteria for the development of a preservation electronic image format would include the following:

1. Capture the image at the highest possible image quality.

2. Store the image in a lossless or minimum lossyness mode based on specific guidelines developed for specific content material.

3. Use format, medium, and equipment that meets national and international standards.

4. Make the format itself accessible on standard equipment (downloadable to other devices) for various levels of access, i.e., display or browse.

5. Create files capable of being stored on standard archival quality medium.

- Highest Possible Image Quality
- Lossless or Minimum Lossyness
- Specific Guidelines Must be Followed
- Meeting National and International Standards
- Tested to be Acceptable with Preservation and Access Mission
- Lend Itself to be Accessible (Device Independent)
- Preservation Quality Storage Capability

Figure 5: The Preservation Format

THE MEDIUM

The medium of interest for the storage and retention of records in digital form is the optical medium. Optical media have been shown to be more durable than magnetic media, and the longevity and expected life issues of optical media seem to be more understood. Furthermore, libraries are acquiring more and more materials already on CD-ROMs. Formats other than CD-ROM are also used for digital or electronic documents. These include magnetic tape, disks, cards, or a combination of the three. These are simply referred to as computer file or machine-readable files. To date, the emphasis in research has been on the CD-ROM and its generation (mastering).

The two questions about CD-ROMs that most concern preservation professionals are: How can the existing CD-ROMS in library collections be managed, especially in view of the fact that these are the only media on which the intellectual knowledge is recorded, and can CD-ROMs or other optical disks be used as a preservation medium or format?

The Library of Congress has developed a working paper on dealing with CD's or other electronic media in machine-readable collections. The paper takes a very practical approach in that all aspects of the systems that support the media and their presentation need to be considered. Once the decision is made that a given title is of "preservation quality," the document is assigned to a preservation category based on the level of effort to be expended in order to keep machine-readable components of the computer package functional. It is not just the package that needs to be in good shape; it is all required support systems, CPU, operation system, drives, players, display devices, and any interactive software. It is not just the CD; it is all the supportive parts to deliver to the user what they want.

Maintaining the functionality of a machine-readable collection is a management issue. Everything cannot be maintained forever in its original format, but with appropriate bibliographic control the users will know what packages are available in working order.

Using CD-ROMs or other optical media as preservation formats involves reformatting the source document. The first part of this paper deals with the testing and decision making necessary to define the file structure and logical order. Questions regarding the longevity of the optical media are still not all answered, but a lot of work is going on in this area.

TESTING OF THE OPTICAL DISK

Medium testing for optical disks has been going on for some time. The testing has been basically for the two most frequently used, the 12 inch WORM (Write Once Read Mostly) disks and the 120mm (4.7 inch) CD discs. The Library of Congress has performed some preliminary testing using both the 12 inch WORMs and some limited testing with the CDs. NIST (National Institute of Standards and Technology) has also tested 12 inch WORMs. These results have been published without any alarming reaction. Work is still in progress and will continue on a low effort with the CDs. This work is focused mostly on the glass "CENTURY" discs made by DigiPress, but with limited longevity testing of polycarbonate discs.

The testing attempts to answer not only how long the disks will last, but what are the failure modes, what causes them, and how to detect that failure is about to occur. Testing is done in a non-destruct manner to as much as possible simulate aging. The Arrhenius aging methodology is the scheme commonly used. This has been written up in numerous reports by LOC, NIST, and X3 standard groups, which endorse the procedure. Care should be given not to induce stress in simulating aging.

The Arrhenius test methodology subjects the sample to elevated temperatures and humidities, then measures deviations of certain parameters after these bakes (typically thousands of hours). The bakes at elevated temperatures must be long enough to get some change in the sensitive parameters. These bakes are done at at least three temperature levels in order to extrapolate to room or ambient temperature.

Testing involves looking at certain physical and electrical parameters associated with the disk. Bit and block error rate are the parameters most often used since they are easy to monitor and usually will indicate that the disk is approaching its end of life. Reflectivity also is often used.

ISO specifies many measurement standards for the CDs and on a complete testing system all these should be measured. There are machines that do this. Maximum acceptable levels are indicated. Although some are more critical than others, users should be aware of these complex procedures and have equipment to perform tests periodically.

The end of life is defined as the time one of an item's importance parameters has degraded to: 1) a point where the disk becomes unsuited for use, or 2) to a measurable point predefined as "end of life" for that parameter. WORMs and CDs handle this differently. But in each case a procedure is defined.

Visual inspection is also very important, but sometimes a disk that looks good will be bad, and a bad looking disk will be perfectly okay. Procedures can be developed and used as a screening tool.

OPTICAL STORAGE AS A PRESERVATION MEDIUM

There are many good arguments for optical disks to be considered as a preservation medium. (See figure 6.) They are well accepted in the market place. This is very important. It is not a short-lived technology. But there are still some unresolved issues. First, the longevity testing is still uncertain. The question is whether the Arrhenius methodology adequately simulates aging. Some feel it doesn't, and work is underway to better understand accelerated aging for optical storage technologies. The second is that there are many manufacturing variables in the production of optical disks that can easily be varied (intentionally or unintentionally) without the user knowing about them. The variations can occur from batch to batch. The effect can then be a defect, or a change from the standard, without the user being aware of the fact. Quality control is very important and must be monitored, from batch to batch and from manufacturer to manufacturer. Currently there are too many "proprietary" processes, chemicals, and techniques for the user to be certain of what they are getting.

Some Issues:

- Well accepted and penetrated in the market place with millions of drives in use.
- Longevity testing still uncertain with more aging testing to be performed on the wide variety of discs.
- Disc manufacturing has many chemical processing variables tightly controlled by individual manufacturers, many of the schemes proprietary. Users are not sure of what they are buying.
- There is no disc certification process to "certify" that a given disc meets certain standards. What does a "guarantee" really mean.
- Access systems to the discs are still in a large part not uniformly accessible. Systems lack interoperability.
- Driven control electronics lack error correction reporting activity for users to monitor system performance.
- ...But there are many positive features and these problems can be solved.

Figure 6: CD-ROM as a Preservation Media

And finally, there is no certification process that a given disk meets certain criteria. Manufacturers "guarantee" disks but from a preservation point of view that is not enough. Adequate certification criteria still need to be established.

Then there is the equipment or the drive. It must have sufficient error reporting features to adequately monitor system performance. Disk drive manufacturers are currently working on this.

Currently these issues are being investigated either formally through standards committees or informally in SIGs. The electronic document system with optical storage still has many positive features and the problems can be solved.

CONCLUSION

The computer industry is a dynamic industry, continually upgrading itself. The industry has a mentality of replacing the old with the new. New systems are better, faster, and cheaper, performing the job or application better. The data on systems need to be maintained, and maintenance is done using migration procedures. If the data are important, upward compatibility is critical. In a sense these same procedures can be used to preserve the data captured in the document image capturing process. The image data are much more complex than text data, and to ensure that the data can always be retrieved and displayed as required, following generations of upgrades, is the major challenge.

If the preservation community is to use this technology as a preservation medium, a case for preserving material on computer files must be made. First, optimum formats need to be defined and standardized. Second, the medium must be of archival quality. And finally, the equipment must always be available to read, access, and display the files as they were intended to be displayed. User requirements are driving standards to be developed to provide users with standard procedures for capturing, processing, storing, and retrieving image documents. Standards are also underway for testing, monitoring, and calibrating systems. These activities are moving quickly. It will continue to be a dynamic process, just like the industry, but it will be the management of the process that will maintain and preserve the collections.

Discussion

Q. I suppose we should begin to consider the format of materials as they're published and added to our collections in terms of whether we will be able to scan them at a high resolution, if we wish to preserve them electronically?

A. Yes, and that is a policy decision as to what formats are scanned and added to the collection. How valuable is the document? Do you want to scan it? The highest possible resolution would be strictly a technical decision...above a certain sampling rate you're not going to add any more information to your image. The most important decision is what image format is used in storing the scanned image.

Q. But the higher quality level will be more cost effective as time goes on?

A. True. That means this scheme gets bigger and bigger and the cost of scanning gets less and less. But I think we have to define what the highest possible image quality is and then decide whether you want to do that. But I think that has to be done. Below a certain point it doesn't make any difference, and you might want to back down from that and decide, this is what we're going to use. I think you have to go through that exercise to define what the maximum scan resolution should be for specific tapes of documents, or even paper.

Q. My question concerns the idea of trying to establish standards, JPEG, lossy mode, and how libraries will come to deal with all of the various options.

A. Sure. I indicated that JPEG gives us a lot of options in terms of capturing and displaying images. We need user guidance to help the user determine the best compression rates for a particular type of image. I'm chairing an AIIM standards group doing this.

Q. Well if various options are utilized, what is the copy of record? Is it the browse copy the casual user gets, or the archival copy, and what does this mean for copyright considerations?

A. The issue is your preservation copy, as I mentioned. I said you want to capture at the highest possible resolution as a preservation copy, but you may not want to distribute it to a user at that level. You want options, to download it to users based upon their requirements or their need, to have it at a certain image quality. You still have it captured and saved at the highest possible resolution quality, and you can always reproduce it at that highest possible level. You might not want to always do that, but that's the option JPEG gives you.

Q. But why limit the quality of the file that we make available to users?

A. I'm not sure that the user always needs the highest possible quality of the image. Browsing, through images in a low resolution mode is faster and cheaper. This may be adequate for the user until a final image is selected for whatever purpose.

Q. Are you concerned about the effect of color or black and white images in terms of what quality is made available to users?

A. The user has the option. They might want to look at a lot of images fast, just in black and white. Or the user might not have a color monitor. JPEG uses a YCrCb color plane, Y is your black and white, Only the Y plane can be transmitted for display—saving a lot of time. The need for color varies a lot with the types of documents and the application. Color must be maintained, but in some cases the user may want the option not to display or print color.

Q. Isn't one of the issues in the presenter quality that we can capture the quality, related to the actual incredible scale of the source materials? The difference in size?

A. That's what your document taxonomy or document type is all about. Different types of source material would define these parameters as a function of your original document, and the size of your original image is one parameter.

Q. It makes it incredibly simple to maintain a high standard of resolution for small items, and incredibly difficult for something large. That's kind of an arbitrary characteristic that can be mapped in the process.

A. Yes. It depends again on what is an adequate form of presentation? What resolution do you really need? Keep in mind also that compression is becoming more efficient, and cost of storage is becoming cheaper.

Q. So, it depends on a user?

A. I think to resolve some of these decisions, or to come up with consensus of what is done, we almost have to get some user input into what they feel is optimal, and from the preservation quality, what is good. We really haven't started to apply some of these things yet.

Q. Could you talk a bit more about reproduction of data and refreshing data?

A. Both reproduction of data and refreshing data in a computer system is a simple management issue or process. This process is commonly done in any system. The problem is, on a long term basis, can we be sure the refreshing will always be done. How can we be sure that someone later on (10–50 years) will decide that a certain collection will not get "refreshed?"

Q. So refreshing is just recopying?

A. Well that's the way I would use refreshing. I don't use the word refreshing, but yes, I guess that's what you would use it as, recopying. It's called migrating your data.

Q. But isn't it true that there is some mechanism such that if data is starting to degrade, copying backward will restore it?

A. Yes, data that are stored on disk, magnetic disk or optical disk use a scheme known as, a detection and correction algorithm and they add information to your file in a redundant mode. They write more data than are actually there, redundantly, so if you do lose some data on your file, that data is picked up from other sections on that disk and your data correction algorithm puts all those bits back in the right order before it comes out to you. It takes your bit string, chops it up in blocks, adds some extra stuff, scrambles it around, because if you lose a block you'll lose a whole bunch of data, so it's better to lose a little piece here, a little piece there. Then they can figure out what's lost, and nothing really gets lost. That's basically the concept. And that's done for magnetic media, optical media, any kind of data storage device. What happens, when you start to read that disk and you find out that your error correction algorithm is working at a certain rate, that means you're starting to lose some bits. It isn't critical yet, you can lose quite a few before you have a fatal error. But when you start to lose these bits, it's now time to transfer the data to another drive. So it reads everything and puts everything in its original form because that's how it comes out of the drive.

Q. Is any progress being made on producing holographic CD's?

A. Have you seen any yet? Maybe Mark Arps of 3M might want to talk to you about it? No, he's shaking his head, too. You may see proteins on a little chip first.

Q. You led us through a very complex description of preservation formats. Would you comment on where average libraries and librarians will be involved in deciding on these formats?

A. I think you will get involved in making decisions in terms of what levels of lossness you will be able to tolerate. If you're dealing with color, if you're dealing with JPEG, you need to make these decisions. You may want to have the manufacturer decide all that for you. It will keep it simpler, but then you become tied to the manufacturers process.

Q. Where do we get the opportunity to make these decisions?

A. When you start using color compression codes, when you compress color or continuous tone images and when you use JPEG. That is where this whole thing will have to fall in place. It's pretty complicated, deciding what is the maximum resolution, what is the maximum image quality you want, or the highest image quality you want —and what access copies you want to have available. And this again, goes back to your taxonomy—for what types of documents? You can't have a general rule for all documents. Certain documents, 300 dpi is good, some 600 dpi is not good, you've got to go higher than that, so, why scan everything at 600? The system should be intelligent enough to select the level that is best for the document.

About the Author

Basil Manns is a Physical Scientist with the Preservation Directorate at the Library of Congress. His primary interests are in developing electronic imaging storage and retrieval systems in support of the preservation and access mission of the Library of Congress. He has spent almost 25 years in the field of electronic image processing, starting his career in a Navy Research Laboratory developing digital image processing schemes, and moving to the Research and Development Office of the Environmental Protection Agency in the field of remote sensing and image analysis before coming to the Library. He has been with the Library for about ten years, focusing on imaging systems and issues relating to document image management.

He is also involved in AIIM standards activities, currently chairing the Image Compression Committee, and is on the Technical Advisory Group (TAG) for ISO/TC-171 (Micrographics and Optical Memories for Document and Image Recordings). He graduated from Valparaiso University with a BSEE and from the University of Maryland with a MSEE in electrical engineering.

5

CD-ROM: Archival Considerations

Mark Arps
Marketing Manager, CD-ROM
3M Optical Recording Department
3M

I hope, in this paper, to clear up some of the questions that you might have on optical media in general, and then to cover more specifically the life expectancy of CD-ROM. I really like the title for this talk that appeared on the program, "the disk that will not die." I'm not sure where it came from, but it's very interesting. In general, I think CD-ROM will live up to that. I have to clarify that my intent is not to try to convince anybody to use CD-ROM for archival purposes or to prove that that's available. I'm just going to give you some additional background to let you, with your expertise and your understanding of the requirements, make the decision on where CD-ROM and optical media in general fit in your electronic preservation strategy. With that, I'll get into a little bit of what I would call on optical media overview.

OVERVIEW

When you think about optical media, your first question might be, why would you want to use it? At 3M, we look at optical media as having these four attributes: removeability, capacity, random access and durability. Take any of those away and you may want to use something else. Without the characteristic of removeability for example, you'd probably end up with a hard drive. Hard drives have very high capacity random access and work quite well. Take away random access and it might be a tape device. You will want to consider what attributes you want, because optical is not the solution for every problem and shouldn't be considered as such.

Another attribute of optical media and the one reason you might choose to use it, is low storage costs. (See figure 1.) Consider costs per megabyte for several formats: First, removable hard disk, (a Bernoulli cartridge); $15 per megabyte; hard disk at $10 (really on-line storage is very expensive); paper at $4 per megabyte; floppy disk, $1.70; microfiche at $0.76; magnetic tape at a little over $0.25; WORM or Write Once optical disks, $0.12; CD-ROM at $0.02.[1] Here CD-ROM comes out the winner, with the caveat that this was for at least 100 copies. For one copy, CD-ROM can be very expensive, but if you have a distribution need, it really fits in quite well.

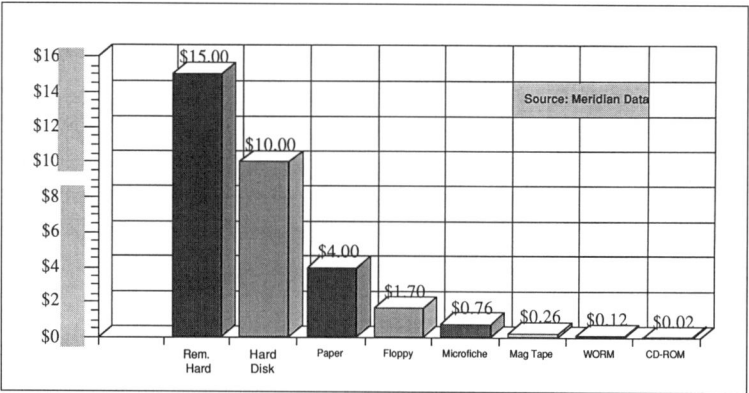

Figure 1: Media Comparison Chart (Cost Per Megabyte)   © 3M 1992

WHAT DO YOU NEED FOR OPTICAL DISKS?

The first thing you need to create optical disks is a laser diode; before there were lasers you couldn't have optical disks. You also need to have an optical head that can focus and track. This technology is only about 12 years old. The optical data storage industry owes a lot to video disks and movies, because that is where this technology was developed back in the 1980s. Finally, at the bottom, you need a laser sensitive surface that specifies function: the disk. (See figure 2.) What makes a disk writable or read-only or otherwise is the disk—the drives themselves are all very similar. In summary, you need a laser, something that can track it, and a disk that is designed to store data.

The way an optical disk stores such large quantities of information is shown in figure 3. On the left of the figure, is the laser beam, which starts off fairly large, about a half millimeter in size; and narrows to a point when it is focused on the data on the disk, at this point it is about a half micron in size. Compare that to a human hair at 75 microns and a cotton fiber at 150 microns. This gives you an idea how small the laser is on that disk and why a CD-ROM can hold as much as it does. That is also part of the reason why it's sometimes hard to read and why, if you damage it, a little scratch covers up a lot.

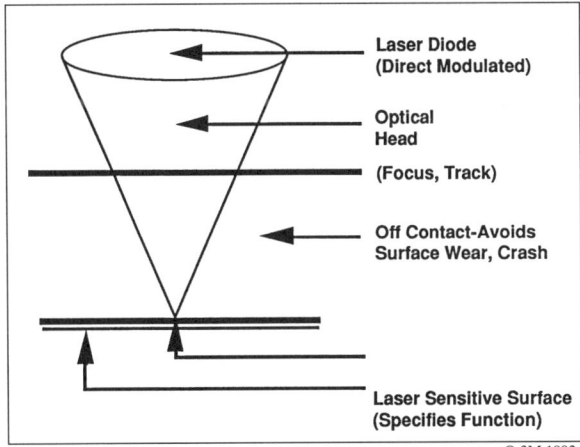

© 3M 1992

Figure 2: Basic Principle of all Laser Optical Storage

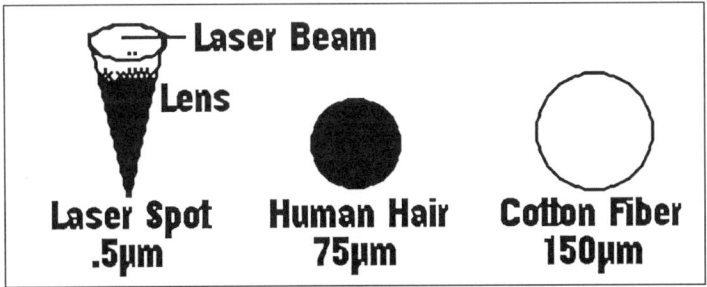

Figure 3: Relative Size of a focused Laser Spot © 3M 1992

WHAT TYPES OF OPTICAL MEDIA ARE THERE?

In general, there are three types of optical media: read-only memory, WORM optical, and re-writable. Read-only is a general category, of which CD-ROM is a specific example. (See figure 4.) There are other read-only memories and I'm sure there will be more in the future. Next, the WORM optical, which really equals write-once. When you use those to scan a document to an optical disk, it is normally to a write-once disk. Again, WORM is an example of write-once-read-many. Basil Manns (Chapter 4) noted that early in 1984 they didn't work very well. We used to call them write-only memory. You just about had to have somebody prove that it was written on. And a lot of times you couldn't; you'd write it, and you'd never get it back.

The newest type of optical memory is called re-writable. It looks quite a bit like a removable hard drive, but the difference is that there's an optical disk inside instead of a magnetic disc. Re-writable optical disks are actually erasable and reusable. It's been tested, you can read and erase it up to 10 million times. I don't know anybody who's going to wear it out.

> • **Read Only**
>   - CD-ROM
> • **Write Once Read Many (WORM)**
>   - Many Formats
> • **Re-writable (R/W)**
>   - 130 mm ISO
>   - 86 mm ISO

Figure 4: Optical Media Types

STANDARDS

CD-ROM is now very standardized. However, for write-once, there is really no standard available, though some are being developed. On the re-writable side, there are standards; it is an ISO standard disk that you can put in many drives. Let me generally mention WORM and re-writable disks. WORM has been around since 1984, re-writable since 1988. In general WORM and re-writable discs are two-sided, you've got to take them out and flip them over instead of using a jukebox to do it. You can store 600–800 megabytes on a 5 1/4 platter. A big 12" WORM platter stores in the one to five gigabyte range.

ISO disk standards exist, but there's really no file standard. This means even if the disk meets the standard, if you write it on a Macintosh, you really can't take it to a PC and read the data. You could reformat and erase the disk and use it on the PC, you just cannot use that Macintosh data. So the standards are developing, but are not completely interchangeable between platforms yet.

PROS AND CONS OF WORM AND RE-WRITABLE

The pros and cons of using WORM and re-writable versus CD are that both of the former are faster in access time and data rate than CD. (See figure 5.) The user can add or modify the data, which is good for small scale distribution (anytime you make five to ten copies). The cons are the lack of standards, and the expense of the drives—on the order of $5,000–$10,000 versus $500 for a CD-ROM drive. Each disk must be individually recorded. There are those who propose using this kind of technology for replacing CD-ROM, but you must consider that it takes two hours to put all the data on each one. Making a hundred copies would be quite time consuming, and they are really not cost effective for mass distribution.

```
• Pros
 - Faster Access Time/Data Rate
 - User Can Add/Modify Data
 - Good for Small Scale Distribution (<25)
• Cons
 - Lack of Standards (WORM)
 - Drives/Media More Expensive
 - Discs Must Be Individually Recorded
 - Not Cost Effective for Mass Distribution
```

Figure 5: WORM/Rewritable

WHAT IS RE-WRITABLE?

Re-writable media can be best looked upon as a hybrid; it's an optical disk and you use a laser, but you store the bits magnetically, which is important, in that it can be erased by a magnetic field or heat. It works by focusing the laser on the optical surface and heating up a small surface area. (See figure 6.) Because of a magnet on it, it flips the bit one way or another, and that is what stores the information. To read it, the laser is focused on the disk again, and because there is a magnetic field, it rotates the laser beam. It's a little bit different, actually quite a bit different, than a WORM or a CD-ROM in the way it reads, but it still uses a laser.

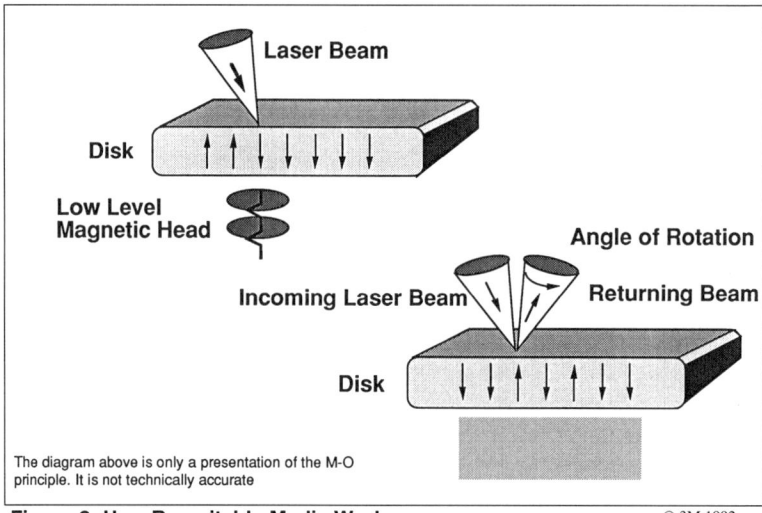

The diagram above is only a presentation of the M-O principle. It is not technically accurate

Figure 6: How Re-writable Media Works   © 3M 1992

WHAT IS CD-ROM?

CD-ROM was introduced in 1985 so it's still a fairly new technology, but it has come quite a way since then. It is a pre-recorded optical media at this point, and it cannot be user recorded. It has a 680 megabyte capacity. The disk itself is produced under a standard that was proposed by Phillips-Sony. It started out as a private standard that they called the "yellow book," which has since become an ISO standard. The technology of how to make the disk, how big it should be, and how to make the drive play that disk is well known. CD-ROM has gone to the next level; in addition to having the disk standardized, it has standardized the files. The standard is the ISO 9660 file standard, which some people call High Sierra. This means that you can take a disk and put it into a Macintosh and read the files, put it into an IBM-PC and read the files, put it in a Cray super-computer and read the files. It does not mean that you could run those files, but at least you can get at them. To run the files you must still deal with the software issue. Finally, another thing about CD that people are somewhat confused about is what I call application standards for CD disks. They define how to put the data on the disks. These include CD-I, if you've heard of CD Interactive. DVI, which is Digital Video Interactive, is for movies, essentially a video on a CD disk. There are also CDXA and CDTV. The next one you'll hear of this summer is called CD-Photo, which is putting photographs on a disk, which Kodak's going to do. I guess the important thing to remember is that they are CD. That defines the disk itself with a standard behind it.

PROS AND CONS OF CD?

Obviously CD has high capacity, since it is possible to get audio, video and data on the same disk. The disk hardware and file system are all standardized, and it's all quite inexpensive. The lowest price drive I've seen just recently is $199 for an external CD-ROM drive. That's really getting quite inexpensive, considering they were priced at $1000 three or four years ago. The costs have really come down in that time.

On the negative side, to put video on a disk we also need to put compression on it, which requires algorithms. JPEG is an algorithm for images that is described by Basil Manns; there's a group called MPEG that is looking at motion picture compression and creating that standard. By definition the disks are fairly slow for access time and data rate, but it is my feeling that it really only comes into play when people are trying to compare CD's to a hard drive, which really shouldn't be done anyway. To access data on a CD may take less than a second, and for people who are used to using microfiche it's as if they've died and gone to heaven, while a computer person will thumb their nose at a second in access time. CD-ROM is not modifiable by the user, which can be a con in certain cases, but probably for libraries, it is actually a positive thing that people can't edit the data.

Storage capacity is, of course, a plus for CD-ROM. If you compare one CD-ROM to a file cabinet full of pieces of paper, the CD could hold 340,000 pages of text. (I have to clarify since I don't want to get Don Willis (Chapter 6) in trouble, that this would be text without any images. Another comparison would match 1800 flexible disks, and again, one CD-ROM; or one CD-ROM can replace sixty-two 50 BPI magnetic tapes or two of the new tape cartridges that are being used. It provides a very high storage density compared to typical magnetic media. Why be concerned about this? I guess for libraries, to some extent, because it is becoming a very popular media. There are about three million drives in use this year. Actually that's a conservative estimate; it's probably in the range of three to five million and growing at a rate of 40% a year.

To summarize where we are with CD? (See figure 7.) We have quite a few standards on the disks, media and the drives; and we have the yellow book which is now ISO standard 10149, the file system, so files can be read off the disk in a standard drive.

- **Pros**
  - 680 MC of Digital Data
  - Data, Video, and Audio on Same Disc
  - Standard Disc, Hardware and File System
  - Small, Inexpensive Hardware
- **Cons**
  - Video Requires Data Compression
  - Slow Access Time/Data Rate
  - Not Modifiable By User

Figure 7: CD-ROM

IN THE FUTURE

The next step people are working on is indexing and retrieval. Some people call these interoperability standards. They are standards that are driven by different industries and different interest groups. The first one is CDRDX CD-ROM Data Exchange, which is being driven by the federal government, actually a segment of the federal government in the intelligence community. Their thought is to have a defined standard for how data is indexed on the disk. Ideally, you could take a disk and have a disk format and standard retrieval system for it, which could be supplied to every government agency. You wouldn't need a different set of software to access Census data than you would to access geographic data or any other type. That is the goal they are working towards.

The second interest group is ATA. The ATA 100 standard is being proposed by the Air Transport Association. They are going to put maintenance manuals for aircraft on CD-ROM. The problem they have is the same one I mentioned earlier. They don't want Northwest Airlines to have fifty different computer systems for every make of aircraft that they have, for every aircraft engine or whatever, so they're defining a standard so that everybody that makes disks in the aircraft industry essentially uses a standard for the way they enter data on that disk. This really has implications for this kind of audience. As standards get further developed we can really begin to see that there will be a defined standard for indexing data in the future. Right now, they're pretty new.

HOW IS DATA ENTERED ON THE DISK?

I want to get back to the disk, and how the data ends up looking on a disk. The data is found in tracks and little pits about a half micron large, essentially starting from the inside out in a continuous spiral on the disk. The pit dimensions are shown in figure 8. Again, if you put a single human hair on there, it'll cover up a hundred tracks. Figure 9 gets into the whole issue of error correction and why CD in general is quite reliable. Looking at the top bar of the figure there are 2048 bytes of user data. It could be images or text or audio or anything. When we at 3M put it on a CD, we add 16 bytes of header first on the front, which lets us find that block of data.

The last part, the 288 bytes on the other end is called EDC and ECC. It's the error detection code and error correction code which is added onto the data. It is added during manufacturing. It gets further complicated by the next process, during which that block is chopped up into 98 different pieces, and essentially scattered all over the disk. As Basil Manns (Chapter 4) mentions, you don't want all the data lined up because if you scratch the disk, you don't want to delete the data all in one piece. This data is spread out all over the disk, so if you scratch it, little pieces that are deleted in any block can be put back together by the ECC (Error Correction Code).

One thing 3M did to be sure the error correction would actually work was to drill a hole in the disk. People who make disks can do that, while people get nervous about doing that in a library. Actually on a CD-ROM disk we found you could have about a 1/16" hole or a little less and it would still play through that. On a CD Audio disk you could actually get up almost to 1/4" before your ear can hear it. It's surprising how bad our ears are compared to the audio disk. The error correction on CD is very powerful, so you can get away with a lot.

ERRORS ON CD DISKS

Every disk manufactured has errors on it as does every floppy disk and every magnetic tape. The user, however, normally isn't aware of it. In figure 10 you can see that the track pits have little black defects between them, the little mark there could be a scratch or black dirt or anything. This is to show that these do effect the read-back pattern, but in general, the computer can figure out the error and correct it. That'll work until the defects get so high in number that the error corrections can't fix them.

One of the problems alluded to in Basil Manns article is that most drives don't report back how many errors they're fixing. This can in effect be like having blinders on and essentially permit you to drive off the edge of the disk. Data will continue to work, especially on audio disks. Audio disks will work until one day, they won't work at all. They don't get noisy, it's error correction overload

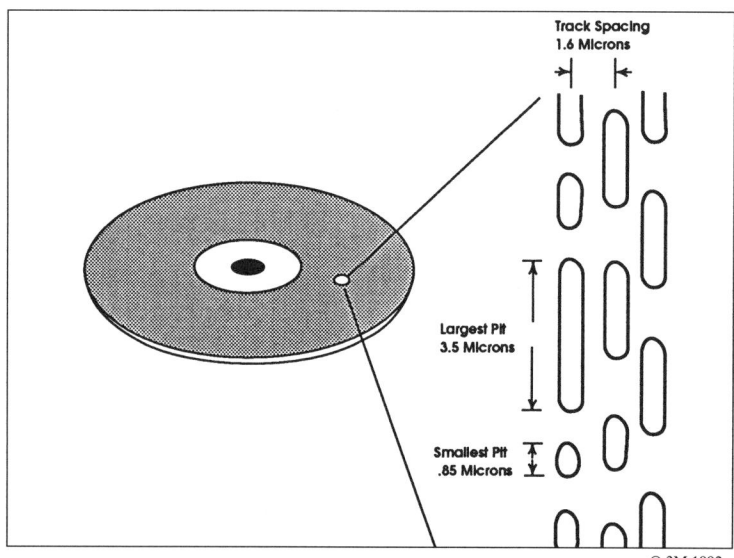

Figure 8: CD-ROM Pit Dimensions © 3M 1992

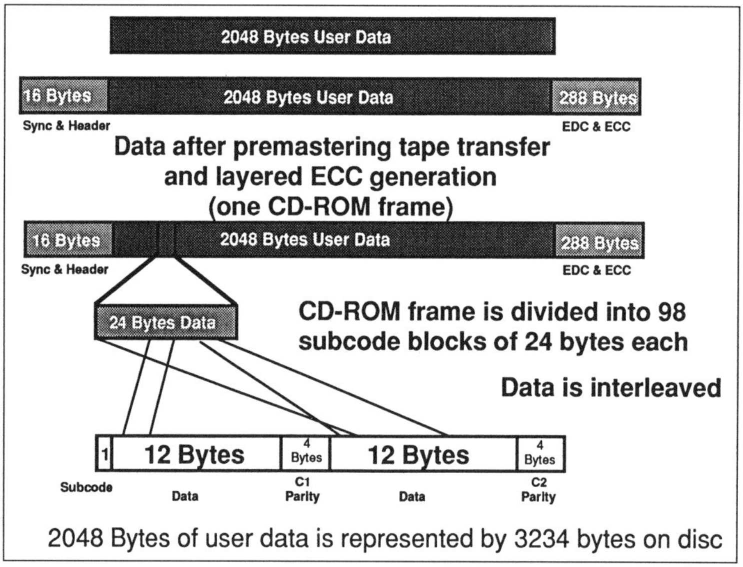

Figure 9: CD-ROM Data Path © 3M 1992

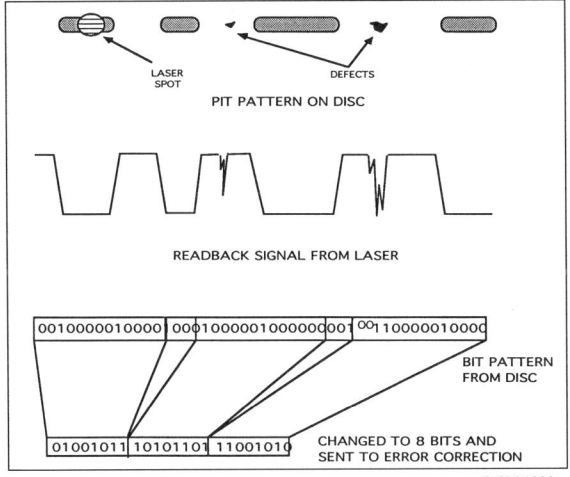

LASER SPOT

DEFECTS

PIT PATTERN ON DISC

READBACK SIGNAL FROM LASER

0010000010000 0001000001000000001 0011000001000

BIT PATTERN FROM DISC

01001011 10101101 11001010

CHANGED TO 8 BITS AND SENT TO ERROR CORRECTION

Figure 10: Reading the Data © 3M 1992

and they simply stop. It is very important in this kind of scenario to have a player that reports back how many defects it's fixing—that gives you advance warning, to replace or refresh the data. There are some expensive drives we use in manufacturing that report this, but there is not currently anything generally available to the public with this capability.

HOW ARE CDS MADE?

Manufacturing the CD is the easy part. Scanning, imaging, and indexing are the hard part that you deal with every day. (See figure 11.) The source data scanned is normally indexed with certain retrieval software, essentially copied by a piece of media by 3M onto the CD-ROM. I have to clarify that speed isn't really the most essential part. A lot of people look upon CD-ROM as magic but it's really a large floppy disk, and can be explained in very simple terms. It's not very hard to make one on your own—all it takes is computer data and software and some way to get it to a manufacturer.

The other major consideration is that most people think that somehow CD's cost $10,000 apiece. I wish that were true, unfortunately it's not. In general, figure 12 shows what a standard CD-ROM job might cost at any one time. The data formatting is really putting the data into the ISO standard we talked about. Mastering, replicating, packaging—in general for 100 disks this would cost about $1500 or $15 a piece.

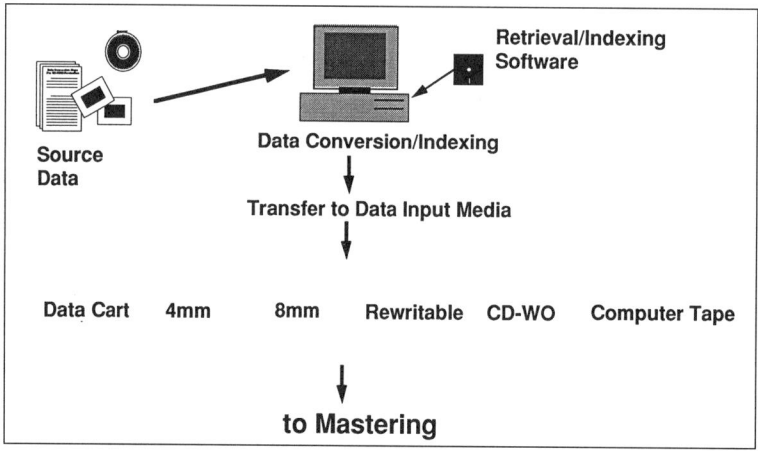

Figure 11: Data Conversion for CD-ROM   © 3M 1992

Data Formatting	$300.00
Mastering (10 Day Turnaround)	$1,100.00
Replication (100 @ 1.40 ea.)	$140.00
Jewel Box Package (100 @ .30 ea.)	$30.00
Total	$1,570.00

Figure 12: CD-ROM Mastering & Replication Costs

WHAT IS INVOLVED IN MASTERING?

Figure 13 shows something about the process itself. 3M's definition of mastering is to take the input data, shown on the left; run it through a laser beam recorder; and laser cut the information, the pit pattern we talked about, onto a piece of glass. The product is our "master." For the next step, we cut those tracks and pits on the master, then go and make what we call a stamper.

Essentially, we are taking a glass indentation and ending up with a piece of metal with bumps that are a half micron in size. That completes the stamping process, which is somewhat complicated. Simplified, it's like putting chrome on your bumper. We chrome plate the master and pull that piece of metal off to make a stamper. In the replication process, the stamper is put into a molding machine. The plastic is actually molded with those indentations in it. This is an

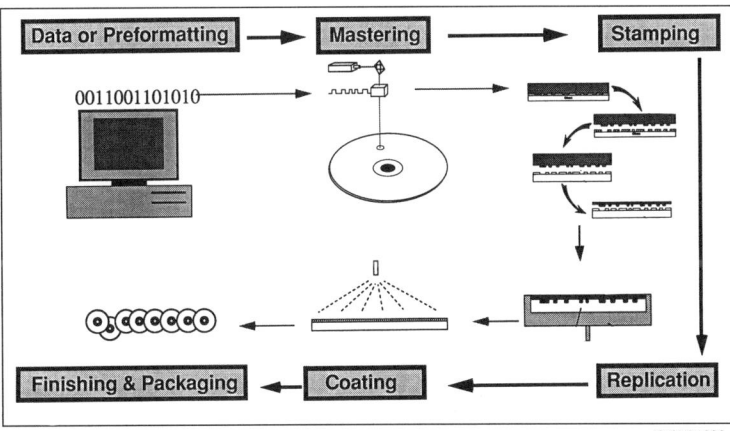

Figure 13: Process Flow

© 3M 1992

important thing to understand. CD-ROMs are physically replicated, not recorded one by one like a magnetic tape is. They're stamped out like cookies—like record albums. This is one of the reasons they are so playable. Their manufacture is a physical thing, not electric, not a magnetic field, or any of the other types of storage. They are molded, then coated with aluminum or a reflector layer, and packaged out.

ACCURACY

Something we're always concerned about is assuring the data is recorded accurately on the CD. Data is sent to 3M in the form of computer tape from a VAX computer or other hard ware source. 3M adds the error correction to the supplied data. That data is recorded onto the master which is on glass. The disk is inspected by a laser for 100% data compatibility.

Once the first copy is stamped off the line, it is taken back and compared byte for byte to the magnetic tape. The quality control cycle is in there to make sure that the data that sent to 3M is byte for byte compatible—exactly comparable to the data on the CD-ROM. That still doesn't catch everything. A fellow at MIT once sent us a tape with all zeros. It made 600 megabytes of zeros. We copied that exactly. It doesn't catch everything. We duplicate 100 percent.

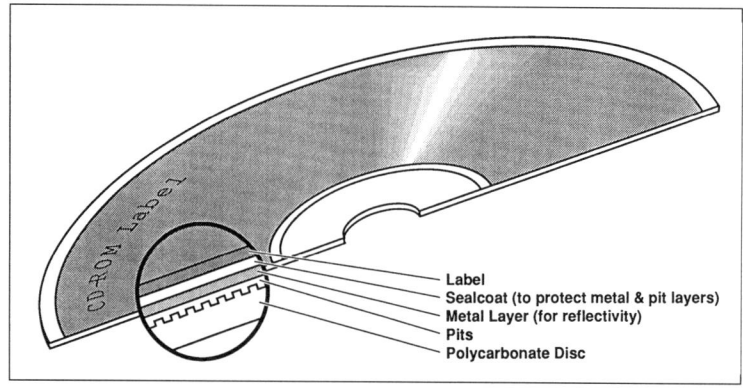

Figure 14: CD-ROM Construction   © 3M 1992

LONGEVITY

We'll get into a little bit of what causes longevity or lack of it. Figure 14 shows how a CD is put together. A CD is a single sided disk, not like a WORM or a re-writable disk which has two sides. The figure is drawn with the label side on the top. Starting at the bottom, in sequence you have the polycarbonate disk, that's the thickest layer, 1.2 mm thick. Molded in that are the pits, which are very much out of scale in the figure, these are in the nanometer range and this scale is wrong, you normally wouldn't be able to see them. On top of the pits and filling them in is the metal layer which makes the disk shiny. That metal is coated on in angstrom quantities so it is also very thin. On top of the metal and as a seal coat, we lay a plastic finish to protect the metal against scratches. Then the label is put on top of that.

It's a multi-layer construction. There are several important elements in this construction, but the seal coat is very important. It covers the inside where there's normally no metal, and the outside where there shouldn't be any metal either, it works as a complete envelope of coverage. When there's a fault, normally it is that the seal coat doesn't cover everything and something gets in.

Concerning handling, I'd say about half the people I tell this to are surprised, the most sensitive side of a CD is the label. Don't scratch the label side. Don't write on the label side, don't put a sticker on the label side, don't do anything to that side. It is the most sensitive side because, if you look at the detail in figure 14, the label is closest to the metal, really the closest to the pits, and you can most easily damage this side. You have to be very careful about

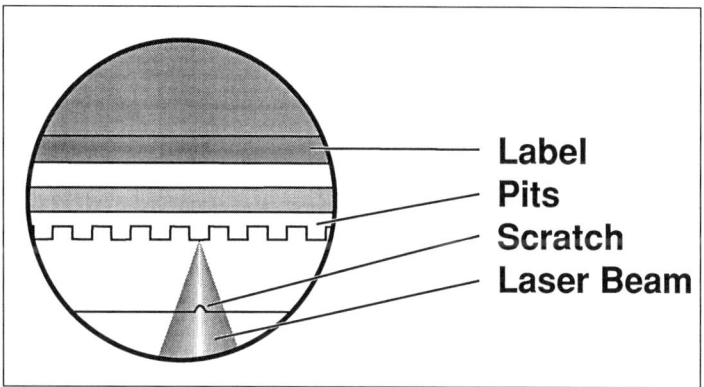

Figure 15: Laser Focus Diagram   © 3M 1992

scratching or cleaning or whatever. If you have a disk that has gone out of print or is no longer needed, an interesting experiment is to take the point of a pen and stick it into the disk. Then look on the other side—you can see it come right through; it doesn't take much. You have to be very careful about the label. And that goes for any disk; audio, ROM, or otherwise.

I would also suggest, for best care and handling, that if the drives you're using in the library are caddy-based, put every disk in a caddy and seal the caddy. Have the ownership marks on the caddy itself and not on the disk. You solve a couple of problems—you don't have people handling the disks themselves, with the danger of fingerprints and scratches, and you've got something that's really robust. Potentially you can put tattle tape on the caddy itself, again, not on the disk.

Looking at figure 15, I want to expand on why the read-side is not as sensitive. From the bottom, the laser beam is shown coming up in a triangle and through a scratch. That scratch is actually pretty big. But what happens is that because the laser is big on the outside of the disk, again about a half a millimeter, it focuses right around the scratch, but still reads the data. If you're a photography buff, focusing through a chain link fence is really good comparison, you really don't see the fence. This is what the disk is going to do with the scratches on the read-side label. Unfortunately that's not as clean cut as it ought to be sometimes either, because if you have a scratch that's circular, sometimes the drive will follow it. The drive thinks that that's where the data is, and tries to follow that scratch around, which will take it off the data trail. That brings up the next recommendation—if you have to clean a disk, number one, don't use any solvent, don't use anything but a soft cloth, and two, don't scrub it in a circular pattern. Go from the inside of the disk out, across the disk. If you scratch a disk in a circular pattern you have a tendency to make tracks that the drive will think are data and it will follow the scratches right off the edge. In general, the best way to clean a disk is not to. I've heard from people who want to use alcohols. Using anything like that is really putting the disk in danger.

With this background, we can discuss the lifetime of disks. 3M was really inundated a year ago with calls from people asking us this question after the *Wall Street Journal* had an article that basically said all CD-ROMs were going to go away in a year. It caused a lot of concern, but the problem was, we couldn't answer the questions, other than to say, we think they're going to last. There wasn't any lifetime data on an obviously new technology, and until then anyway, there weren't any studies. 3M started a study, and what we found is good news, bad news.

The study included several types of disks, both audio and ROM from different manufacturers, and of course, 3M. They were put in an environmental chamber and baked. The disks were baked at 60 degrees Celsius and 85% RH. Looking at figure 16 you can see the axis indicating BLER increase. BLER is block error; it identifies drop outs, or defects, on the disk. We found that some disks over time, some almost over night, became unreadable, after only 24 hours in the chamber. This shocked us and a lot of other people too. For us, the good news was that our 3M disks lasted the longest and did the best in this chamber. But again, with only one condition tested, this really was not a very controlled test. We still couldn't answer all of the questions generated by the *Wall Street Journal* article.

We did learn more about what happens to the disks. The best disks didn't have any degradation at 7500 hours; others showed areas where there was supposed to be just shiny metal, but in the middle the pits started which indicates the data is degrading. With a disk that should be shiny metal, but instead has little pock marks running up into the metal, the player is unable to tell a pit from a pock mark, and will not be able to read the data. It overloads the error correction system and makes it fail. Another interesting finding is that every disk had its signature—some had little pock marks, some had a lot of big ones. In general, every manufacturer has a little different process, and so the failure mode is a little different also.

Comparing what a disk should look like and what a disk looks like after it has degraded, demonstrates a couple of things. First, disks degrade from the outside in. This indicates that the seal coat didn't seal very well, because some-

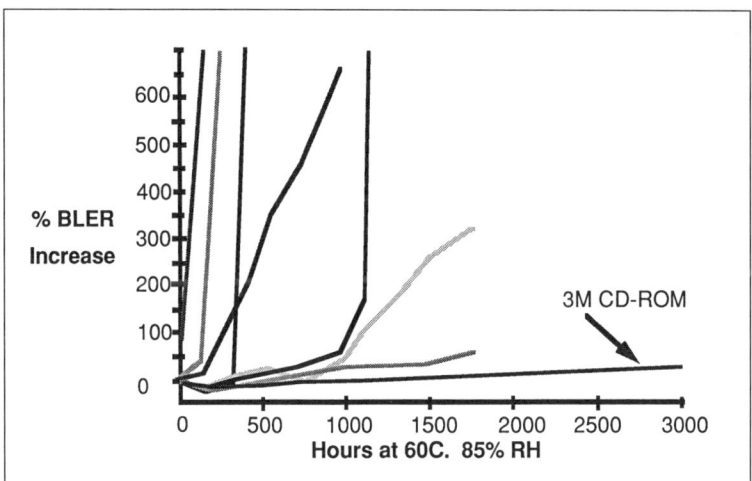

Figure 16: CD-ROM Manufacturers Durability Comparison   © 3M 1992

thing is seeping in from the outside. Secondly, we noticed visible white circles scattered around. We call these pin holes. One of the problems that users have is knowing how to tell whether a disk is good or bad. One thing you can do, is take your disk and hold it up to the sun, or put it on an overhead projector. If it looks like it just got shot with a shotgun, that disk is probably not going to last very long. Or, if the metal is very thin, if you can see your hand through it, it probably won't last long. Generally, you shouldn't be able to see your hand through the disk. If you can, and I would bet more than half of the disks in your library are in this state, the lifetime is going to be fairly short. I've seen disks so thin that you can put them on an overhead projector and project the label onto the screen. We had a couple that turned out like this. There's really no metal left at all. These make very good Christmas ornaments, but other than that, they're useless.

WHAT EFFECTS THE WAY DISKS DEGRADE?

There are several factors which effect the degradation we saw. Some of these are materials issues: what kind of plastic you use, the metal itself and how pure it is, (there are different metals called 4 nines, which is 99.99% pure and metal they call beer can aluminum that's not), and the seal coat and exactly how it is applied. Another factor, one which is less prevalent today than it was early on, is problems caused by printing the ink label on the disk. Over time, because the ink wasn't compatible, it would actually eat through the disk. That hasn't happened recently. Manufacturing methods, as I alluded to, also effect the way disks degrade quite a bit. One thing is initial error rate, obviously. For all disks, the error rate goes up over time, as you accelerate age, so the lower the rate to begin with, the longer the disk lasts. There's quite a bit of range in the initial error rate. Temperature and humidity and storage all make a difference in longevity. That's a large factor in any storage strategy or any preservation argument. Storage and handling are important. Scratches are a result of just how you handle the disk.

As a further follow-up, we did what we consider the most complete study done to date on CD-ROM. We selected a sample of disks in nine different test chambers with varying temperature and humidity and baked them for 4000 hours (about six months) and then did the calculations and analysis on those disks. The figure shows the conditions that we used in nine different chambers, ranging from 80 degrees Celsius through 50 degrees Celsius, with relative humidity up to 85%. (See figure 17.) This is designed in what statisticians call the box square. To predict lifetime, you can do it with one chamber, but then you have very limited data. Do it with several chambers and you can compare the data and try to figure out which condition effects longevity—the temperature or humidity. If testing is done in just one chamber, you don't know which condition caused the results. Data over time looks somewhat like this, with the error rate starting at about two to three errors per second and ending at about the same range, maybe a little higher, at five errors per second. (See figure 18.) Compare that to the industry specification for this error rate at 220 per second, and we're quite a ways away from that even for our internal spec. This demonstrates the importance of having initial errors be so low, and how that effects lifetime.

Accelerated Lifetime Testing Cells						
Cell #	Temp ˚C	R.H.%		Cell#	Temp ˚C	R.H.%
1	80	85		6	70	75
2	80	75		7	60	85
3	80	65		8	60	65
4	80	55		9	50	85
5	70	85				

Figure 17: Accelerated Lifetime Testing Conditions

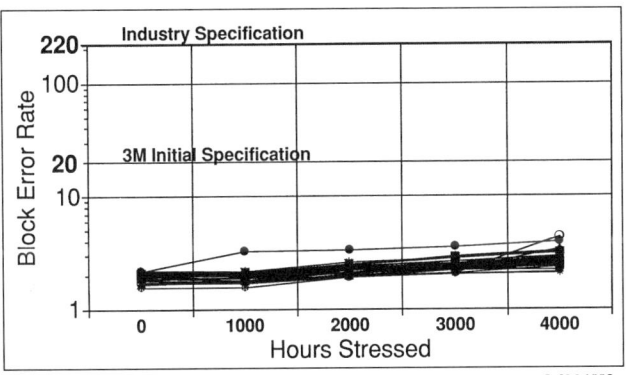

Figure 18: CD-ROM Lifetime Study Results

© 3M 1992

I'm not going to explain the equation in figure 19. It is the Eyring model. There are four dimensions to it. 3M felt it was most applicable to this lifetime study. Tomorrow, our test methods will be proposed when the ANSI committee discusses a standard for determining the lifetime in years of optical imagery. I think that one of the things we want to do is to make this a standard and use it so you can certify how long a disk will last. There are actually some proposals about putting the letters LE for Life Expectancy on the disk. A disk that is marked LE-10 indicates that the manufacturer will guarantee that the disk has a life expectancy of ten years. Things are moving toward a point where you'll be able to tell how long the disk will last.

$$M = AT^a e^{(\Delta H/kT)} e^{((B_1 = C/T)S)}$$

Figure19: Eyring Model

Putting all the data through the equation resulted in a graph called a survivor function. The statistical ranges shown in figure 20 show 99.6% survivability as the limit; then you take the first graph, where BLER=50 as end of life. It gives you lifetime as a hundred, you have an envelope of 100–300 years. Go out to the end of life at 220, which again, is the industry spec, you end up with a lifetime of 1000, and an envelope of 1000–1500. Clearly one hundred years is a very acceptable lifetime.

The full study is being proposed to ANSI and the results are going to be published in the National Media Lab's newsletter, called *NML BITS*, in the next

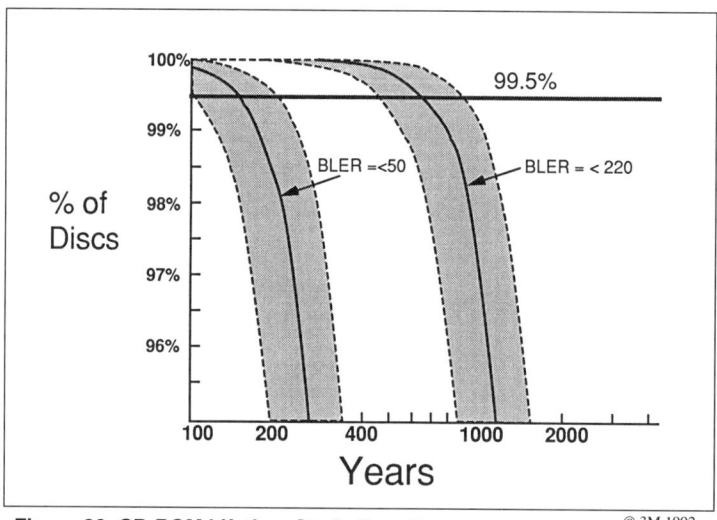

Figure 20: CD-ROM Lifetime Study Results   © 3M 1992

issue. We worked with National Media Lab and the study was announced in March 1992 at the CD-ROM conference in San Francisco.

We'll get to, in the end, what 3M came up with. Under specified operating conditions of a disk, which are up to 70 degrees Celsius, 3M decided on a warranty of 25 years, that we feel takes into account temperature fluctuations. We know the disk will last a hundred years at room temperature, so 25 years takes into account fluctuation. Now again, rapid fluctuations from 80 degrees Celsius to liquid nitrogen at zero causes problems, but general storage fluctuation, as long as it's non-condensing will easily allow longevity of 25 years. The last bullet in figure 21 is something I have to say (lawyers make me say it), actual lifetime will depend on your own usage and storage.

- 99.5% of Discs Readable
- Stored at 30˚C/90%RH
- BLER (Block Error Rate) <50 errors/second
- >100 Year Lifetime
- Actual Lifetime will depend on your own usage, handling and storage conditions.

Figure 21: Lifetime Statistics Prediction

So again, 3M ended up with a 25 year warranty that assures 100 year lifetime at room temperature. The 25 year warranty entails a wide variety of temperatures and is available on a 3M spec sheet.

Some issues to consider: the disk, as other people have said, is only a third of the problem. (See figure 22.) Another third is software, including what operating systems are going to be around in 10 or 25 years. I don't know how many versions of DOS we've gone through in the last five years, but quite a few. We have OS/2 and UNIX. That is a real consideration. The nice thing is that the file format is defined, so in theory anybody with a new operating system would write a driver to access the disk, but it's not guaranteed.

The last issue obviously is hardware. (See figure 23.) In terms of compatibility, the standard has been pretty well established. Positive points include that there are multiple manufacturers, ten or twelve. It's hard to guarantee availability, but one of the positive things is that CD-ROM does have a strong consumer electronics base versus any piece of industrial equipment. WORM drives, tape drives and such will never have such a strong base. I forget how many CD players there

- **File Format**
    - ISO9660
- **Operating System**
    - DOS
    - OS/2
    - UNIX
- **Indexing Scheme**
    - CD-RD$_x$
    - ATA 100

Figure 22: Software Issues

- **Compatibility**
    - Philips/Sony "Yellow Book"
    - Multiple Manufacturers
- **Availability**
    - Consumer Electronics Based
    - Multiple Manufacturers
- **Interface Standards**
    - SCSI

Figure 23: Hardware Issues

are, but there are in the range of 500 million CD-ROM Audio players out in the world. CD-ROM players are based on the CD Audio so, there's a base there that's not going to go away overnight, which I think will help the CD-ROM availability over time.

The last thing is interface standards. Most CD-ROM drives are hooked up with what's called SCSI, which is a really good standard for interconnecting equipment. It will be supported for quite some time.

In conclusion, CD-ROM is highly standardized, probably the most standardized media with the exception of 9-track tape, maybe even more standardized than 9-track tape. The media itself can last for one hundred years plus, but issues remain in the hardware and software areas that'll have to be addressed in the future.

Notes

1. The source of this data is a CD-ROM services company called Meridian Data.

Discussion

Q. Could you clarify a bit about the mastering process? Do customers send raw data, or has the information already been through an imaging process before the CD-ROM manufacturer receives it?

A. The information I presented about mastering all assumes that we're getting data already imaged or scanned or whatever on a magnetic tape. Really like I say, making the CD is the easy part, the hard part is the data provider has to furnish the data in the proper format.

Q. So if the data was scanned already the costs would be less?

A. Yes, well it would be less, but the mastering would be the same. What you would really have, if you look back at figure 12, you would have $14 there instead of $140. The mastering is the large cost. That's why I say CD-ROM isn't really cost effective. In general, compared to other media, you normally consider the crossover about 50 copies. If you look at a floppy disk being, what did we say before, a dollar something a megabyte, normally a floppy disk holds about a megabyte. A dollar a disk. If you have over 50 megabytes of information you would and should put it on a CD-ROM.

Q. Go back to the construction of the CD for a minute. The coating is a polycarbonate? Or is that the plastic?

A. It's really a multi-layer construction. The plastic, what's called a seal coat protective coat is on top. It's not necessarily a polycarbonate. There are variations between manufacturers.   Normally today, it's called a UV-cured polymer, a hardened polymer. Early on in some of the early CD's it was actually an air drying furniture polish, which didn't work very well, but normally today it's a hardened polymer that covers the disk.

Q. A lot of us were surprised by what you said about labelling CD's, but I'm sure a lot of us have the same concerns and the same questions about how we can put some sort of ownership marking on disks. Even though it may not be good to do, we need to mark these disks.

A. Yes, that's a problem. If you need to put anything on the disk, I would use a permanent magic marker and write in a circle in the inside hub. Don't write anywhere over the metal. That can have the tendency of scratching the metal or in the case of sharpie markers or whatever, it can actually eat through over time.

Q. So essentially we're writing on the label? On the label side of the disk?

A. No. The only place you should, if you need to mark a disk at all, is in the hub area, just the clear area where there's no metal. Not on the label at all. Anything on the label can potentially damage that disk. Or, on the packaging or on the caddy would be my recommendation, but you really have to be sure that people don't scratch the label side. But I've seen people when they take disks out of drives, throw them on the desk label side down, because they think they're protecting the other side. Really, if anything, you throw it read side down, the other side is thicker anyway.

Q. There are a number of disk cleaning products offered commercially, through catalogs and such. Which are the best? Do you recommend any of them?

A. I wouldn't use any. You've heard of snake oil? I don't know, and I can't say we've tested everything, but in general, again, not knowing what people put in their disks, every disk is different from a chemical standpoint, materials standpoint, and you don't know if that cleaner is compatible. It's best to use a soft cotton cloth and a photograph negative cleaner, a little puffer brush to get dust off. Really the best way to keep fingerprints off of that is by maintaining disks in a caddy if you can. They're going to last the longest that way.

Q. The testing you described for longevity seemed to only take into consideration a few variables. How reliable are the results of that testing? Could you go into a little more detail about the testing methods?

A. Well, there's a lot of reliability theory that I don't claim to know, but in general, in order to predict lifetime you have to do accelerated aging, which in general, is elevated temperature and humidity, and monitor the changes over time. So you monitor the rate of change, then you bring that down to room temperature and say well, at the rate of change at room temperature, how long will that last? Really, it's the only way to guess how long they might last, other than waiting around a hundred years or so.

Q. Some of the disks that are offered for sale have a gold surface. In your testing, did those fare better than others? Are they of a superior quality?

A. I've heard people say because they put gold on disks they'll last a hundred years and that's simply not true. Unless you do the tests you can't tell. Really the gold doesn't make a difference.

Q. At one point in your talk you mentioned using an overhead projector to look for pin holes in disks. Isn't that damaging to the disks? I'd be afraid the heat, overheads get really hot, could damage the plastic.

A. Oh, to hold it up to the light? No. That won't hurt the polycarbonate. You're not going to leave a disk on an overhead for long.

Q. I have a question about the Eyring equation and the impact of fluctuations in temperature and relative humidity. Did you do extensive testing of various changes in temperature and RH?

A. We really didn't. I would agree that fluctuations, quick fluctuations are a problem, but in general, fluctuations over time aren't as big a problem for CD as they might be for magnetic tape. But only quick fluctuations, for example, if you take a disk that's been in a chamber at 80 degrees Celsius, and throw it in liquid nitrogen it explodes.

Q. I'm concerned about the humidity factor. Many libraries have air conditioning problems, at my library the AC is only turned on during the day, so the humidity varies.

A. That's a problem. As long as it's non-condensing, it won't be a problem for CD-ROM. If it's condensing you have all kinds of problems. Water droplets on anything are going to create problems.

Q. What about air pollution and it's effects on CD's?

A. We really didn't look upon that. But obviously, any corrosive chemical or anything in the air is damaging.

Q. You talked about tattle tape systems a little bit. If we desensitize a disk that's been tattle taped, are we going to risk losing data or damaging the disk in any way?

A. Magnetic fields and such don't have any effect on it. No. There's nothing magnetic in it.

About the Author

Mark Arps is a graduate of UW Madison with a degree in electrical and computing engineering. He joined 3M first in 1981 in the optical recording and manufacturing division in the plant in Menomonee, Wisconsin where UW Stout is. He spent six years in the optical disk manufacturing line and has held a variety of positions. He is currently with their main plant in St. Paul, Minnesota. Since 1988 he has been responsible for coordinating the worldwide marketing effort for CD-ROM.

6

The Resolution Factor in Preserving Page-Based Materials

Don Willis
Director of Advanced Technologies
UMI

Designing the future digital image system to preserve deteriorating print materials means making a number of trade-off decisions. Undoubtedly the most important factor to consider is resolution. It is impossible to make informed choices involving quality versus cost in a digital image preservation system without understanding the resolution trade-offs.

Unfortunately, the combined use of photographic and electronic technologies in today's micrographic imaging systems has made both the use and interpretation of the term "resolution" complex. Generally, resolution is defined as the ability to accurately render spatial information. It can be assessed in rather finite terms by using known test targets as comparisons. (See figure 1 on page 110.)

There are two other variables that will affect resolution. They are contrast and granularity. Contrast is the lightness difference between a feature and its immediate surroundings. It can vary from 5:1 to 100:1. Anything greater than 12:1 can be considered high contrast and that lower than 3:1 is considered low contrast. Resolution is always stated in terms of high contrast targets. The second variable is granularity(noise). It is the amount of unwanted light fluctuations, or noise, that distort an observer's ability to perceive the image's resolution.

Contrast and granularity are interrelated by the following rules:

1) If the image contrast increases and the noise remains the same, resolution increases;

2) if granularity (noise) increases, and contrast remains the same, resolution decreases. The ratio of contrast to noise is commonly referred to as the

signal-to-noise (SNR) ratio. If SNR increases, resolution will follow. If SNR decreases, so will resolution. [1]

But how many, if any irregularities, can be tolerated when defining the image preservation system resolution ultimately depends on the individual circumstances. The amount of data being captured (resolution), type of materials, font sizes, as well as the overall project objectives, affect the preservation system's design. If the intent is only to preserve the information content of the page, it can be accomplished at a much lower resolution than would be required to provide a high fidelity replica of the original.

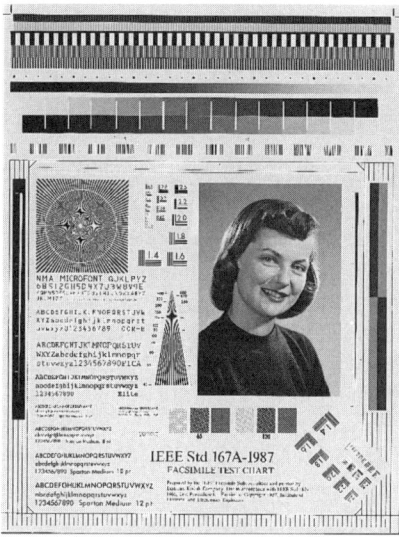

Figure 1: Test Target

ARCHIVAL RESOLUTION

For instance, archival resolution can be defined as about 600 dots per inch (dpi) with eight bits of gray scale—or as high as is economically and technically possible at a given point in time. It should prove adequate for preservation work and should provide a completely faithful reproduction of the original document. Adequate resolution could be defined to be about 300 dots per inch (dpi) without gray scale (binary). This lower level of resolution should preserve about 99.9 percent of the page's information content. It is adequate for providing access to preserved information. The digital image preservation system designer should aim to achieve the optimal balance between minimal system cost and maximum image quality—whether the page ultimately is stored on film, optical disc or some other media.

To make an everyday comparison with these standards, the typical facsimile machine is transmitting at a resolution of 200 dpi. At this level all but the smallest type fonts and finest lines are faithfully, albeit crudely, rendered. Although there is a good deal lost in the halftone areas of the page, most of the intelligence of the page is preserved. Therefore, by scanning at the adequate resolution, which is 50% higher, one can expect that some of the continuous-tone or halftone information, along with some of the detail such as small fonts or fine lines, will be lost. But there should be little difficulty for the user to recognize the characters—which is why today's fax machines are so useful and popular.

Obviously one of the first steps the system designer should take is to examine the material that will be preserved. How old are the documents? How do they vary by font types and background coloration? Should the artifacts on the documents be preserved or eliminated? A random sample of the material should be compared with some resolution test targets to assess the smallest fonts that must be captured. The document should be scanned in a test mode and displayed on a high resolution monitor at the original resolution. Portions can then be magnified, right down to the individual character level, to see if the characters are being formed properly. Other important system design criteria include the workload volume, quality required, methods for storing and accessing the documents, frequency and urgency of access, response-time requirements, condition of the documents and page sizes.

FILM RESOLUTION VS DIGITAL RESOLUTION

How do film resolution and digital resolution interrelate? Film resolution is defined typically as the number of line pairs per millimeter that can be resolved. A line pair is one dark and one light line juxtaposed. Simply stated, a series of line pairs is considered resolved if all lines in an array on a test target can be identified reliably. Film resolution is measured by photographing several test targets and determining the smallest target on which the individual lines can be differentiated clearly.

A digital image is analogous to an electronic photograph. It consists of a series of dots or pixels that can be represented in computer memory by a digital code. Digital image resolution is measured in the number of these dots sampled per inch. Typical scanning resolution available commercially is between 300 and 600 dots/inch. The number of samples is governed by the resolution of the digital image scanner. The image itself contains no intelligent data. Therefore, the dots can be used only to recreate a representation of the original. The higher the resolution, the higher the fidelity of this recreated representation.

It should also be noted, though, that because these digital dots are very small, a great deal of them are required to recreate the image. For example, at a resolution of 300 dpi, 90,000 dots per square inch are generated. This means that large amounts of storage space are required to maintain high-quality image data.

Theoretically, microfilm is capable of storing resolutions of 1,000 line pairs per millimeter, but even the best microfilm cameras operating under ideal conditions are limited to about 200 line pairs per millimeter. Further limitations due to lighting, exposure control, lens quality, focus, development chemistry and other variables in a production environment mean the average film is usually imaged at an effective resolution of about 140-150 line pairs per millimeter. This would equate to a digital scanning resolution of approximately 800-1,000 dots per inch (dpi) without gray scale. Cost-effective, off-the-shelf digital image systems capable of handling this level of resolution under production conditions will not be available for a few years.

A preservation system designed today around only digital image technology must be configured to solve three major problems. One is the lack of a true archival storage capability, the other is the need to scan at high resolution, around 600 dpi with gray scale, to create an archival quality image; and the last is the high cost of archival resolution image storage on optical disc.

A preservation system based on micrographics technology alone, which follows all the standards for the creation, handling, processing, and storage of the film, will capture documents that will be preserved for hundreds of years. The most obvious drawback with micrographics as a storage media is its lack of access capabilities.

However, today's technology has become sophisticated enough to allow the development of the hybrid preservation system. The hybrid system allows the designer to take advantage of the strengths of both film and digital. The major advantages of film are its standardization, relatively low cost, and archival storage characteristics. The major advantages of digital are its strengths in providing access and its transmission capabilities.

In a hybrid system, the practitioner can choose to either film first and scan the film (See figure 2), or scan first and create film from the digital input data

Advantages:	Disadvantages:
Known technology with familiar document processing requirements	Can't segment the page for optimal quality.
High-speed planetary cameras more available than high-speed scanners.	Low or high contrast only.
Technology currently available.	High-speed cameras are primarily the higher reduction ratio 16mm.
Works well when little indexing or processing is requires.	NARA does not consider 16mm film archival.
	Filming is a linear process while imaging is inherently parallel.
	Quality can only be determined after the fact.
	Scanning from film is a second generation process.

Figure 2: The Film First Option

Advantages:	Disadvantages:
Scanners improving in quality, speed, document handling and cost.	High-speed grayscale scanning requires handling large amounts of data.
Can segment page for optimal quality using image enhancement.	Technology is relatively new and somewhat immature.
Possible to create higher quality film than can currently be created photographically.	Requires powerful processors and large amounts of magnetic disc space.
Digital imaging is inherently parallel.	Higher risk than film first.
Ability to intelligently index film as a by-product of the scan operation.	
Cost sill decrease with time.	
Real time quality determination.	
First generation operation.	

Figure 3: The Scan First Option

(See figure 3). If an institution decides to create film first, the designer may select either low or high contrast film based on the type of material being processed and then optimize the chemistry accordingly. Many experts recommend filming first and then scanning the film. They believe scanning the film may produce better results than working with the original hard copy. Another benefit is that the film can be used for the ultimate archive.

If the choice is to scan first, the key decision revolves around the input resolution. Scanning original documents at a yet to be determined optimal archival resolution, which is believed to be around 600 dpi with eight bits of gray scale, allows for the production of the highest quality, most cost effective preservation images. Optimal resolution in this instance means a balance that offers image quality comparable with photographic methods, while minimizing the amount of data stored. This high quality digital data can be used as input to an electron beam or digital computer output microfilm (COM) camera to produce film, the quality of which is governed by the scanning resolution and amount of gray scale data captured.

As resolution increases, the quality and fidelity of the resulting digital image improves. The time required to scan and process the image, the amount of data captured, and the storage space required also increase in direct proportion to the increased resolution. Certainly a high resolution archival system must be designed with more powerful processors; higher capacity communication channels; more random access memory (RAM), magnetic disk storage capacity and scanners; and possibly custom hardware to handle the compression, decompression, and processing of high resolution images. Likewise, the capital costs and operating costs for a digital image preservation system are directly proportional to the resolution it is designed to handle. It is believed then that the hybrid system offers the practitioner the best options for both preservation and access, and that film should remain the ultimate archive for some time to come.

As one can see, the resolution decision in any digital image preservation system is absolutely critical. Not only will it affect the system's design, but it also determines the maximum possible quality for each image captured. The bottom line is that the system designer has to have a clear understanding of how much image resolution is required, not just desired, as well as how quickly the technology will advance and the costs decrease. He or she must design to maximize resolution within current and future cost-effective boundaries.

In addition, the preservation system should be modular, easily expandable and extensible. It should anticipate future technology advances. Although many would appreciate high technology and wizardry as part of a state of the art system, it is not a necessity in every instance. But neither should that alternative be ignored. Planning and designs incorporating digital imaging into the preservation system actually could, and should, begin as soon as possible.

Notes

1. Williams, Don, "A Tutorial on Photographic and Electronic Imaging Resolution," AIIM Technical Report (TR26), unpublished draft.

Discussion

Q. What is required for a preservation format to be considered a legal media?

A. I don't know that I can answer that question, but it applies only if you have legal requirements for your collection, for instance, in the law library you may well have those kinds of considerations. There have been some test cases, but I'm not sure exactly where that is right now.

Q. It seems libraries are really chasing technology with all of this. At what point do we decide to go with a given product or scheme, such as scanning equipment, to produce archival film?

A. Well, I think the basic factor is higher resolution and more processing power. The only thing that's limiting the resolution right now is cost. There are scanners available on the market that can go up to 2000 dpi resolution. Those are the scanners that work very slowly and they're fairly expensive. Gray scale is coming along because of the desktop publishing applications. I just think it's a matter of technology moving forward a little bit. I think that you'll be able to create very good film in the 600 dpi area. Maybe it's not 600, maybe it's 800, but it's in that area.

Q. A question concerning the way your data is presented. When you give a figure, 200 dpi or 600 dpi, or whatever, is that straight calculations, or is that interpolated?

A. Yes, it's straight calculations. We really need scanners that operate at 600 dpi or 800 dpi real resolution, not interpolated, and some of the scanners that are in use today really are built to scan at 400 and they interpolate it up, so the numbers can be confusing.

Q. In choosing scanning equipment for purchase, it's important then, that we know in advance what resolution must be achieved for the collections we intend to scan?

A. Yes. That's correct, and I think that gets back to what Basil [Manns] was saying before. You look at the characteristics of your documents, and some of them are going to need this high resolution and some of them aren't. You know, if you're saving office documents or something like that, you're just saving information; then you just want to save it at the lowest optimal resolution possible.

Q. Do you predict that as the technology advances, both higher speed and better resolution will be possible?

A. Absolutely. It's just like the example I gave you with the image enhancement equations that we were doing initially on the 386; at 16 megahertz it took us 25 minutes to process one of those pages. Now running on a RISC processor it takes us 17 seconds. Those kinds of major leaps are very possible.

Q. As a preservation medium though, our major concern has to be that no information is lost, so the quality produced by the scanning has to meet preservation criteria.

A. I think everybody would agree with you. I think that we need both. We need to be confident that the preservation needs are met, and that you're not going to lose anything in the preservation process. At the same time we have to make it accessible to the people who need to get access to it. I think that those requirements will be met. It's just a matter of time— and it's less than five years.

Q. Microfilm is a tried and true media. Scanning and electronic options are relatively new and may be here and gone within a few years, to be replaced by a whole new technology as yet unforeseen.

A. Right. There are no guarantees. It's like some of the things that we're finding, like Mark Arps (Chapter 5) mentioned about the early CD-ROM; you develop a process, you experiment with the process, you do accelerated aging, you do testing, and then you work with the process for a long period of time. We make mistakes. That's probably, the key thing. If I were to think about the problem, I would form the question as follows: How can I create a very high fidelity copy of the page right now, that I can put on some media and have confidence that I can go back there in fifty years or so, and recopy it without any loss or any degradation. And I think that's going to be the key. And maybe that media is the optical disk, because you can recopy it in a lossless way. But we're going to have to start thinking in some of those terms. Personally I think film is a very good media. If you create digital film, very high quality digital film, with gray scale data, I think that you should be able to transfer between film and digital and back again without any loss of data provided you're using only lossless compression algorithms.

Q. With upgrades in technology occurring at such a rapid pace, I have to have some concern over the idea of electronic media for archival storage. It seems there's a real danger of ending up with files and no equipment to access them.

A. Right. You could certainly foresee something like that, but the Archives, when they accept material, as Fynette [Eaton] was saying, make very sure that they have the capability to play them and the documentation that's needed to store them. I don't think that that's the risk. I think the risk is, if all of us go off and do our own thing with regard to preservation, we'll end up with systems that won't play together, and be using things that are non-standard. And those are the kinds of things I think we've got to avoid.

Q. The possibility of creating the high resolution microfilm and then using that as the backup for the electronic files has exciting potential, but aren't there still problems with microfilm.

A. Yes. If microfilm is your backup, there are those who would argue that microfilm has its own problems. For instance, you cannot recreate good halftones from microfilm. We would have to be able to scan it at very high quality and retrieve the gray scale. We have to be able to reproduce a good image. I think it was Basil Manns (Chapter 4) who said that maybe we need to measure things differently. We need to measure the end user quality and not necessarily the quality that's stored on the film because certainly the end user quality of what you can get from digital storage is higher than what you can get from microfilm right now. There's a lot of those issues that we've got to deal with. I agree with you.

About the Author

Don Willis is the Director of Advanced Technologies for UMI. He's been in CD-ROM technology almost from the beginning—ten years or more in electronic imaging and CD-ROM publishing. He has general research and development responsibilities for electronic data on CD-ROM at UMI and he worked at the Library of Congress in one of their first digital image document storage and retrieval systems back in 1982. Don is a member of ALA, the American Management Association, the Association for Computing Machinery, IEEE, AIIM and he is a member, among other things, of ALA's Electronic Imaging Technology Committee and AIIM's CD-ROM Task Force. He has two master's degrees, one in computer science, one in business administration.

Conclusion

Janice Mohlhenrich
Preservation Librarian
Marquette University

Summation might be a better description for this portion of the proceedings than conclusion, for the word conclusion implies some sort of finality. In this case, these proceedings, although a window onto current thought about electronic preservation and preservation of electronic formats at a given moment in time, describe a dynamic process. By the date of publication of this volume and in the days to follow, more work will be done toward standardization, more progress will be made on the projects described by the speakers, and new products will be designed and marketed by manufacturers of hardware and software. Meanwhile, in libraries throughout Wisconsin and across the country, irreplaceable books and documents become brittle, are damaged through mishandling or neglect, or are replaced by soon-to-be-obsolete formats, a situation only too familiar to any who may still own 8-track cassette tapes but find no machinery available to play them.

A number of messages are clear. Librarians at all levels must educate themselves so that thoughtful, knowledgeable decisions concerning the care of collections can be made. State preservation agencies, library schools, and publishers of library literature must take an active role in promoting this education. An ongoing partnership must be fostered and strengthened between libraries and the vendors who serve them. Supply and demand systems require knowledgeable consumers if both sides are to achieve satisfaction. *Caveat emptor* applies to CD-ROM products too! We must not allow ourselves to be taken in by fancy graphics and clever marketing if the proposed products do not meet our needs. Appropriateness of a given technology for archival purposes must be proven by careful testing before the technology is entrusted with valuable documents. Librarians must make their voices heard in the development of standards for these products.

The adoption of electronic formats leads us one step closer to realization of the goal of expanding our services beyond the walls of the library. Clear communication is needed as this paradigm shift from individual localized collections to shared access to collections via electronic formats—libraries without "books" or walls—takes place. Let us hope for leadership that embraces the best of new technology while maintaining perspective on the long-range needs of library patrons of the future.

The invention of the codex was of enormous importance to the history of western civilization. It is truly a privilege to experience holding in one's hands a book dated 1550 or 1650...to turn the pages, read the words, and marvel at the transfer of information from mind to mind, bridging the centuries without the need of any other devices to allow understanding. As we make decisions today to develop new technologies for preservation and discuss the merits of various strategies, the concept of hybrid technologies, scanning and filming or creating copies both online and in hard copy, echoes our desire to embrace progress while retaining that which time has proven effective.

All of the preservation strategies, projects, and options discussed in these proceedings require funding. Research and development of new technologies requires funding. Conferences and workshops developed by cooperative preservation programs (like this conference) require funding. In these difficult economic times it is imperative that the importance of libraries be made obvious and that funding be made available. Preservation of our resources is too important to be left to chance or passed over in favor of funding more ephemeral projects. It is up to librarians to beat the drums to call attention to the pressing needs facing our libraries. Preservation of our cultural heritage is a solemn responsibility. We must have funding if we are to succeed in preserving (electronically or by other means) the information housed in our collections. Each of us must recognize the importance of this work and assume responsibility for making our needs known.

The future holds exciting opportunities for the preservation of information. All of us must work together to make the most of the technological advances afforded us. The papers included in these proceedings indicate the burgeoning interest developing as the potential use of electronic formats is considered for preservation. The members of WISPPR hope that this publication will serve to stimulate thought and to educate readers.

Appendix A

Annotated Bibliography on Electronic Preservation

Karen L. Hanus
Reference Library
Medical College of Wisconsin

This bibliography contains references to items that examine the issues and problems of protecting machine-readable records for future use and of using machine-readable media to preserve human-readable documents. The documents cited cover electronic formats such as audio and video storage media, magnetic media, optical media, and electronic mail. The bibliography is not comprehensive. Items which were unavailable for review are not cited here.

Anderson, Michael. "The Preservation of Machine-Readable Data for Secondary Analysis." *Archives*. Vol. 17, no. 74 (October 1985): 79-93.

Report of a seminar held at the University of Essex on February 15th and 16th, 1984. Issues discussed include an overall background of the problems associated with the short life of electronic information, the importance of preserving the documentation of machine-readable data, the problem of choosing the data unit to be examined when data is being sampled for preservation, hardware incompatibilities, and preservation/conservation methods. Although the article does not examine the topics comprehensively, it covers many different problems and suggested solutions associated with the archival preservation of electronic information.

Balon, Brett J., and H. Wayne Gardner. "Disaster Planning for Electronic Records." *Records Management Quarterly.* Vol. 22, no. 3 (July 1988): 20-25, 30.

> The structure of an electronic records disaster plan differs from that of paper records due to the storage medium, its storage requirements, and the equipment needed to retrieve and maintain the information. The article acknowledges that failure to have a disaster plan for electronic records could be devastating to an organization. The authors discuss several elements of a disaster plan including cost-benefit analysis, options for alternate site locations, the action plan, and testing and maintenance of the plan.

Bearman, David, ed. *Archival Management of Electronic Records.* (Archives and Museum Informatics Technical Report #13) Pittsburgh: Archives & Museum Informatics, 1991.

> Contains papers written by Kenneth Thibideau, David Bearman, Margaret Hedstrom, Alan Kowlowitz, Michael L. Miller, and Terry Cook. The essays explore concerns that electronic records may not belong in an archival environment and that archival retention of these records may not be possible. The authors also talk about the appraisal of electronic records.

Bearman, David. *Optical Media: Their Implications for Archives and Museums.* (Archival Informatics Technical Report, Vol. 1, no.1) Pittsburgh: Archives and Museum Informatics, 1987.

> Bearman discusses what videodiscs, compact discs, and optical digital discs are and how they store information. He explains how to decide whether an item of this type is of archival quality. While this paper is meant for the archivist who wishes to transfer paper items to an electronic format, it also may be useful for someone who wants to learn some of the more technical aspects of these electronic storage media.

Clames, Alan R. "Monitoring the U.S. Charters of Freedom by Electronic Imaging." [In: National Archives of Canada. *Proceedings of Conservation in Archives. International Symposium, Ottawa, Canada, May 10-12, 1988.* Ottawa: National Archives of Canada, 1989.: 243-251.]

> Described is the Charters Monitoring System (CMS). In 1987, the National Archives and Records Administration installed a charged couple device (CCD) camera and image processing system to monitor the condition of the Charters of Freedom (Declaration of Independence,

Constitution, and Bill of Rights). The system is able to compare the pattern of one image to another to detect changes that may occur in a document.

Calmes, Alan R. "Relative Longevity of Various Archival Recording Media. [In: National Archives of Canada. *Proceedings of Conservation in Archives. International Symposium, Ottawa, Canada, May 10-12, 1988.* Ottawa: National Archives of Canada, 1989: 207-221.

Calmes explores the life expectancies of paper, photographic film, magnetic media, and optical disks. Frequency of use is one of the most important considerations in choosing a storage medium for information. Reformatting from one medium to another as the demand for the data increases may actually be reducing the storage life.

Carlisle, Van G. "Avoiding Electronic Media Disasters." *Records Management Quarterly.* Vol. 20, no. 1 (January 1986): 42-43.

The article notes the importance of a disaster preparedness plan for protecting electronic data media against fire and other disasters. He acknowledges that off-site storage and backup sites are the generally accepted solutions. He also gives a "mini" plan that can be carried out immediately until a formal disaster plan can be made.

"CD-ROM Disc Maintenance and Care." *OCLC Micro.* Vol. 6 (December 1990): 6.

This brief article makes general recommendations for disc care, cleaning, and protection.

Cuddihy, Edward F. "Stability and Preservation of Magnetic Tape." [In: National Archives of Canada. *Proceedings of Conservation in Archives. International Symposium, Ottawa, Canada, May 10-12, 1988.* Ottawa: National Archives of Canada, 1989: 191-206.]

The author describes experimental aging studies to determine why magnetic recording tapes sometimes become sticky and shed gummy materials. Cuddihy explores the findings which specify safe environmental conditions for tape use and storage.

David, Martin. *Archival Preservation of Machine-Readable Records: The Final Report of the Wisconsin Survey of Machine-Readable Public Records.* Madison: State Historical Society of Wisconsin, 1981.

Contains recommendations to archivists for establishing a machine-readable records program. The recommendations are concerned with prearchival control, appraisal, conservation, security, and access. David identifies problems that archivists still face today and are still learning to overcome. The report concerns itself solely with concepts concerning the archival control of machine-readable records and not with any specific media.

DePew, John N. *A Library, Media, and Archival Preservation Handbook.* Santa Barbara, California: ABC-CLIO, 1991.

Contains a chapter on the preservation of audio and magnetic media. The chapter gives instructions for archival storage and handling of audiotapes and videotapes and identifies potential problems and ways to recover from those problems. It also has lists of do's and do not's for audio and video media as well as for 5.25 inch floppy disks and compact discs. The author included a valuable list of addresses and telephone numbers of preservation services, suppliers, and education programs. The list includes a subject index.

DeWhitt, Benjamin L. "Long-term Preservation of Data on Computer Magnetic Media: Part I." *Conservation Administration News.* no. 29 (April 1987): 7, 19, 28.

The first of this two-part report reviews the physical characteristics of computer magnetic tape and the problems that can occur with the medium. It also reports that recording modes have an effect on the long-term retention of data on these tapes.

DeWhitt, Benjamin L. "Long-term Preservation of Data on Computer Magnetic Media: Part II." *Conservation Administration News.* no. 30 (July 1987): 4,24.

Part II discusses how to prepare tapes for long-term storage, what storage conditions to maintain, and how to sample tapes for read errors. It also gives basic suggestions for retrieving data from damaged tapes.

Easton, Roger. "Conservation of Film, Television and Sound Records." [In: National Archives of Canada. *Proceedings of Conservation in Archives.*

International Symposium, Ottawa, Canada, May 10-12, 1988. Ottawa: National Archives of Canada, 1989.: 163-172.]

> Technical Operations, Conservation Branch, National Archives of Canada manages the conservation of motion picture, television, and sound documents acquired by the Moving Image and Sound Archives Division. Easton addresses concerns with the conservation of original recordings, copying processes, and copying technologies.

Farrington, Jim. "Preventive Maintenance for Audio Discs and Tapes." *Notes: Quarterly Journal of the Music Library Association.* Vol. 48, no. 2 (December 1991): 437-445.

> Farrington describes environmental conditions, equipment, and procedures for the maintenance of relatively good copies of audio media. The author states that the restoration of worn or damaged copies requires the attention of a specialist.

Fox, Barry. "CD Makers Perform in Unison to Stop the Rot." *New Scientist.* Vol. 134, no. 1815 (April 4, 1992): 19.

> Fox reports that CD manufacturers have been meeting to solve problems of short CD lifespan and to establish standards for disc manufacture and testing.

Gavrel, Katherine. "Conceptual Problems Posed by Electronic Records: A RAMP Study." *Information Reports & Bibliographies.* Vol. 20, no. 3 (1991): 15-30.

> The author outlines the problems which electronic records present to traditional archival methods. Machine-readable records pose difficulties for archivists in relation to appraisal, selection, arrangement and description, conservation and access. The author's purpose is to identify issues for further study.

Gavrel, Sue. "Preserving Machine-Readable Archival Records: A Reply to John Mallinson." *Archivaria.* Vol. 22 (Summer 1986): 153-155.

> The author critiques John Mallinson's essay, "Preserving Machine-Readable Archival Records for the Millenia," while examining issues that he did not consider. Gavrel examines how appraisal and conservation enter into the long-term care of machine-readable archives. She also points out that the recommendation made by the Committee on Preservation of the National Archives and Records Administration to preserve machine-readable records by storing them on human-readable

microfilm, which is advanced by Dr. Mallinson, was not accepted by the National Archives and Records Administration.

Geller, Sidney B. *Care and Handling of Computer Magnetic Storage Media.* Washington D.C.: Institute for Computer Sciences and Technology, National Bureau of Standards, 1983.

This paper covers the aspects of the conservation techniques used on computer magnetic storage media. It deals principally with computer magnetic tapes as this was the prevalent mass storage medium used by government organizations at the time this publication was issued. It presents guidelines for the long-term archival storage of tapes including recommendations for the quality of tapes chosen for long-term storage, for preparation of tapes for storage, and for the reactivation of tapes that have been stored. Also, Geller examines the environmental effects on tapes and the effects that exposure to specific magnetic fields and other devices may have on computer media. This publication covers most of the aspects of preservation of magnetic tapes. Although this item was published in 1983, the information concurs with the information scattered throughout more current documents.

Harrison, Helen P. *The Archival Appraisal of Sound Recordings and Related Materials: A RAMP Study with Guidelines.* Paris: UNESCO, 1987.

Harrison gives guidelines concerning what audio items should be preserved as well as how they should be preserved. She also gives suggestions for the method of appraisal and selection for machine-readable records.

Harrison, Helen P. "Conservation and Audiovisual Materials." *Audiovisual Librarian.* Vol. 13, no. 3 (August 1987): 154-162.

The author defines the various audiovisual materials and explains the problems that can occur with each of the media. She suggests that copies of audiovisual items be made and considers the problem that some items cannot be copied. Storage conditions are listed. Harrison also considers which materials should be preserved.

Hedlin, Edie, and Donald F. Harrison. "The National Archives and Electronic Data." *Reference Services Review.* Vol. 16, Nos. 1-2 (1988): 13-16.

The authors discuss the accomplishments of the Machine-readable Branch of the National Archives and Records Administration from

1968 to 1979. They specify the procedures for the care of information stored on magnetic tapes used by NARA such as creating two copies of every data set accessioned. Some of the problems of preserving electronic records such as the absence of standards for data interchange are also discussed.

Hedstrom, Margaret L. *Archives and Manuscripts: Machine-Readable Records*. Chicago: Society of American Archivists, 1984.

Contains information on preparing a machine-readable data file for long-term retention. Suggests sampling stored data files for read errors periodically and reformatting items as the technology changes. Gives an overview of the archival procedures used for magnetic computer media.

Hedstrom, Margaret. "Optical Disks: Are Archivists Repeating the Mistakes of the Past?" *Archival Informatics Newsletter*. Vol. 2, no. 3, (Fall 1988): 52-53.

The author stresses that the records that offices are scanning onto optical disks will soon confront archivists as another information technology problem in the same way magnetic media has. Archivists should become involved in the design of optical disk systems if they are using them to store information of long-term value. Hedstrom emphasizes that archivists need to address new information technologies when they are created rather than waiting until large numbers of records are stored in obsolete formats as happened with magnetic media. She also compares magnetic media to optical media in an effort to identify problems that can be avoided with this newer technology.

Hedstrom, Margaret, and Alan Kowlowitz. "Meeting the Challenge of Machine-Readable Records: A State Archives Perspective." *Reference Services Review*. Vol. 16, Nos. 1-2 (1988): 31-40.

The New York State Archives and Records Administration's Special Media Records Project, which surveyed the nature, quantity, and condition of electronic records in 19 New York State agencies is discussed. The authors describe the criteria and processes that the archives use to select electronic records for permanent preservation. The article includes suggestions of how archivists can improve the management and preservation of electronic records.

Henderson, Kathryn L., and William T. Henderson, ed. *Conserving and Preserving Library Materials*. [Papers presented at the Allerton Park Institute held November 15-18, 1981.] Urbana-Champaign, Illinois:

University of Illinois Graduate School of Library and Information Science, 1983.

> This collection of papers includes information on the preservation of nonpaper materials and a chart which outlines the general physical preservation needs for most nonpaper library materials. It also includes the recommended temperature, relative humidity, packaging, shielding, and inspection frequency. (A 1991 edition of papers presented at the Allerton Park Institute held on November 6-9, 1988 called *Conserving and Preserving Materials in Nonbook Formats* includes more information on the preservation of machine-readable records but was unavailable for review.)

Herther, Nancy. "Between a Rock and a Hard Place: Preservation and Optical Media." *Database*. Vol. 10 (April 1987): 122-124.

> The author interviewed a member from each of two groups which analyzed the information storage media available for archival storage. The Smithsonian Institution Libraries completed a report that evaluated the possible use of compact discs as a replacement for microfilm. The National Academy of Sciences committee studied preservation methods and recommended strategies for helping the National Archives and Records Administration with its storage of documents. The Committee looked at the durability and longevity of microfilm, paper, magnetic tapes, magnetic disks, and optical disks from the viewpoint of preserving information for an indefinite period of time. The problem of rapidly changing storage formats and hardware is emphasized.

Holmes, William M., Jr., "The ODISS Project: An Example of an Optical Digital Imaging Application." [In: National Archives of Canada. *Proceedings of Conservation in Archives. International Symposium, Ottawa, Canada, May 10-12, 1988.* Ottawa: National Archives of Canada, 1989.: 233-241.]

> ODISS (Optical Digital Image Storage System) is a project established at the United States National Archives and Records Administration which involves the digital image capture of paper and microfilm documents. The project examines the processes of the conversion operation including image enhancement and quality control.

Irons Walch, Victoria. "Checklist of Standards Applicable to the Preservation of Archives and Manuscripts." *American Archivist.* Vol. 53, no. 2 (Spring 1990): 324-338.

> The Society of American Archivists Task Force on Archival Standards identified 150-200 standards related to archival preservation. The article presents the standards with information on cost and availability and describes the organizations that developed them.

Irons Walch, Victoria. "The Role of Standards in the Archival Management of Electronic Records." American Archivist. Vol. 53, no. 1 (Winter 1990): 30-43.

> Standards can help archivists to preserve long-term access of information in electronic form. The author describes these standards and the organizations which set these standards.

King, Alan. "The Care and Feeding of Your CD-ROM Disk." *Database*. Vol. 14, no. 6 (December 1991): 105-107.

> The author presents basic guidelines for the maintenance and protection of compact disks.

Lesk, Michael. "Special Section: Digital Imagery, Preservation, and Access." *Information Technology and Libraries*. Vol. 9 (December 1990): 300-306.

> The author examines the alternatives of preserving paper-based materials in their original form, by microfilming and by electronic imaging. Cost of preserving and reformatting, the differences between ASCII storage and image storage, and the loaning of documents in different formats are considered. The author recommends that librarians use either digital imaging or microfilming. Whichever is more manageable should be used now, but it is expected that the digital form will be the choice in years to come.

Levitt, Martin L. "A Case Study in Audio Tape Transfer." *College & Research Libraries News*. Vol. 49, no. 10 (November 1988): 654-657.

> Levitt, the Assistant Manuscripts Librarian at the American Philosophical Society Library, explains the preservation/conservation procedures for the audiotape collection at the Philisophical Society Library. He includes the procedures for surveying the collection, the cost projections for saving the collection, and a description of the equipment needed to create an audio conservation lab.

Lora, Pat. "Preservation or Global Delete? What's the Future of Media?" *Wilson Library Bulletin*. Vol. 66, no. 3 (November 1991): 59-60.

The durability and longevity of compact discs, videotapes and film, and of the equipment needed for their use is discussed. Lora notes that reformatting master tapes requires copyright clearance. The author also suggests that cleaning, periodic inspection, and temperature control might help extend the life of videotapes and audiotapes.

Mallinson, John C. "Preserving Machine-Readable Archival Records for the Millenia." *Archivaria*. Vol. 22 (Summer 1986): 147-152.

Mallinson describes the activities of the Committee on Preservation of the National Archives and Records Administration concerning the preservation of machine-readable records. He emphasizes that the Committee concluded that the archival problems with preservation of machine-readable records are not with the media on which they are stored but rather with the machines which quickly become obsolete. He also explains that the Committee recommended human-readable microfilm to preserve these records.

Mallinson, John C. "On the Preservation of Human- and Machine-Readable Records." *Information Technology and Libraries*. Vol. 7 (March 1988): 19-23.

Mallinson again goes over the Committee on Preservation of the National Archives and Records Administration deliberations and recommendations of July 1984. He also outlines the archival properties of magnetic and optical recording media, of software and documentation, and of hardware.

Mallinson, John C. "Magnetic Tape Recording: History, Evolution and Archival Considerations." [In: National Archives of Canada. *Proceedings of Conservation in Archives. International Symposium, Ottawa, Canada, May 10-12, 1988*. Ottawa: National Archives of Canada, 1989.: 181-190.

Mallinson focuses on audio, video, and computer tapes. The paper discusses concerns about the physical stability of the tapes and the concerns about the long-term availability of the proper hardware for playing and reading the tapes.

Marshall, Mary E., "Compact Disc's 'Indestructibility': Myth and Maybe." *OCLC Micro*. Vol. 7, no. 1 (February 1991): 20-23.

> Marshall examines the suitability of optical media for long-term audio and data storage. An overview of the manufacturing process is given as well as a description of problems and defects that can occur during the process. Suggestions for disc care and for choosing a vendor are given.

Marshall, Mary E., and Ginni Voedisch. "Compact Discs: Permanence and Irretrievability May Be Synonymous in Libraries as Well as Roget's." [In: Williams, Martha E. ed. *National Online Meeting 1990. Proceedings of the 11th National Online Meeting, New York, 1-3 May 1990*. Medord, NJ: Learned Information, 1990.: 249-254.]

> Studies concerning the maximum expected life of compact discs have resulted in conflicting reports. Based on these reports, the authors reconsider the suitability of optical media for archival storage. The authors give guidelines for disc care to avoid CD rot and suggestions for prolonging longevity of discs.

McIver, Glenys. "The ACLIS Working Party on the Preservation of Machine-Readable Records." [Paper presented at the seminar entitled "Punchcards on PCs?—Coping with machine readable records in libraries and archives," held in Canberra in March 1990 under the auspices of the Canberra Online Users Groups of ALIA.] *LASIE*. Vol. 21, no. 2 (September/ October 1990): 37-44.

> McIver reports on the continuing deliberations of the Australian Council of Libraries and Information Services. The Working Party divided the machine-readable records into nine major categories. They are: training packages and educational software, research communities' information exchange, reference type publications, factual files, expert systems, CAD (computer-aided design) and CAM (computer-aided manufacture), authors works in progress, and cartographic records. They focused on four major problems for each type of record: What data elements are worth preserving? How frequently should preservation copies be made? In what form should they be kept? and Where should they be kept? The author also examines the results of the investigations and what the Working Party sees as directions for future actions.

Nelson-Strauss, Brenda. "Preservation Policies and Priorities for Recorded Sound Collections." *Notes: Quarterly Journal of the Music Library Association*. Vol. 48, no. 2 (December 1991): 425-436.

> The author presents a list of appraisal guidelines for recorded sound collections. Some basic suggestions for conservation of audio collections are given. The author maintains that cooperation between libraries to develop preservation programs for audio materials will help librarians to preserve their local collections.

New York State Archives and Records Administration. *A Strategic Plan for Managing and Preserving Electronic Records in New York State Government: Final Report of the Special Media Records Project*. Albany, New York: University of the State of New York, State Education Department, State Archives and Records Administration, 1988.

> The final recommendations of the Special Media Records Project for the improved management and selective preservation of machine-readable records in New York State agencies are presented. Issues which result from increased use of new information technologies such as wider distribution of information in electronic form and diverse forms of software are outlined.

Nowicke, Carole Elizabeth. "Managing Tomorrow's Records Today: An Experiment in Archival Preservation of Electronic Mail." *Midwestern Archivist*. Vol. 13, no. 2 (1988): 67-75.

> Nowicke focuses on the Navy Laboratories History Program's attempts to capture the information in the electronic mail system for the Navy Laboratory archives. She examines the implications of electronic mail for the archivist and the reasons for preserving electronic mail. The article describes the methodology of the Navy Laboratories' study.

Olson, Nancy B. "Hanging Your Software Up to Dry." *College & Research Libraries News*. Vol. 47, no. 10 (November 1988): 634-636.

> The author reports on the recovery efforts of the staff of the Memorial Library at Mankato State University when a leaky roof caused extensive damage to a group of audiovisual materials including a complete run of a software serial. Details of how the water-damaged materials were saved are included.

Osborne, Larry N. "Those (In)Destructible Disks: or, Another Myth Exploded." *Library Hi Tech*. Vol. 7, no. 4, (1989): 7-10+.

Based on a personal experience, the author explains how to salvage 5.25 inch floppy disks that have been damaged by spilled liquids such as coffee, soda, and greasy substances. Included is a step by step list of instructions for saving a damaged disk.

Oudard, Denis. "The Evolution of Century Disc Archival Technology." *CD-ROM Professional*. Vol. 4 (November 1991): 42-46.

The author gives a history of the Century Disc, an archival CD created by Jean Ledieu and his company, DIGIPRESS. A review of the manufacturing process and the research agreement with the Library of Congress to validate the Century Disc's longevity are presented.

Paton, Christopher Ann. "Whispers in the Stacks: The Problem of Sound Recordings in Archives." *American Archivist*. Vol. 53, no. 2 (Spring 1990): 274-280.

According to Paton audio recordings have largely been excluded from the archival literature. The author makes a claim that the reason may be the division of "paper" and "sound" archivists and the lack of communication between the two different camps. Other reasons include the difficulties of appraisal, processing, and conservation that sound recordings cause for "paper" archives. The author offers suggestions for improving the status of sound recordings in archives and gives suggestions of issues that archivists may want to examine when appraising and processing sound recordings.

Richie, Mark. "Videodisc Emerges as a Powerful New Medium...With New Complications." *Sightlines*. Vol. 2 (Fall 1990): 7-9.

Richie explains why videodiscs developed and why they are popular. He also discusses some of the aspects of preservation of videodiscs such as storage and cleaning.

Saffady, William. "Stability, Care and Handling of Microforms, Magnetic Media and Optical Disks." *Library Technology Reports*. (Special Issue). Vol. 27, no. 1 (January/February 1991): 5-116.

The author gives a comprehensive look at the problems of machine-readable data and offers suggestions for how to avoid or resolve the problems. The issues discussed include accidental erasure, print-through, media wear, storage and handling, and environmental effects. The author also gives guidelines for media selection.

Smith, Eldred. "Why Microfilm Research-Library Collections When Electronic Data Bases Could Be Used?" *Microform Review*. Vol. 20, no. 1 (Winter 1991): 27-29.

> This article compares the current practice of microfilming collections to the author's proposal of preserving collections electronically in a database that would be accessible to all research libraries. The author argues that preserving the content of deteriorating paper documents in an electronic database would be faster and more convenient for users. For librarians, the database would eliminate the problems of local maintenance and interlibrary loans.

Stielow, Frederick J. "Ducking the Cutting Edge: Archival Theory and the Preservation of Electronic Media." *The Ohio Archivist*. Vol. 22, no. 2 (Fall 1991): 3-7.

> Stielow covers the basic elements of the preservation of electronic media. According to the author, the archivist must demand standards, plan carefully, and expect new challenges in preservation. He gives suggestions for maintaining the content of the media. He also gives a summary of the work that's being done to institute standards for electronic media.

Stielow, Frederick J. *The Management of Oral History Sound Archives*. New York: Greenwood Press, 1986.

> Contains a detailed chapter on conservation management. Includes recommendations for maintaining the environment in which audio media are stored. The author explores options for maintaining security. Also presented are standards for preservation masters, disaster planning, and types of equipment.

Tissing, Robert W., Jr., "Audiovisual Archives in the LBJ Presidential Library." [Paper presented at the 1990 meeting of the Society of Southwest Archivists, May 17, 1990, in Austin, Texas.] *Conservation Administration News*. no. 44 (January 1991): 1-2, 24-25.

> The author describes the Lyndon B. Johnson Presidential Library and its audiovisual archives. An overview of the guidelines for audiovisual preservation which the archives has developed are given.

"UNC Archivists Bake Some Tapes." *Wilson Library Bulletin*. Vol. 66, (January 1992): 11.

> A brief description of a solution to stabilize deteriorating sound recordings at the University of North Carolina at Chapel Hill is given. The tapes were baked in a cardboard oven with a hair dryer at 122 degrees Fahrenheit. The process stabilized the tapes long enough to rerecord the content onto new tapes.

U.S. National Research Council. Committee on Preservation of Historical Records. *Preservation of Historical Records*. Washington, D.C.: National Academy Press, 1986.

> Overall, the Committee on Preservation of Historical Records is concerned with preserving paper records. There is information on magnetic recording media and optical disk technology, but it is more of an argument to prevent records of these types from being considered archival. The argument examines the problems of items becoming obsolete quickly, the short life span of these media, and the lack of standards for the materials, formats, and hardware for electronic records.

Vogelgesang, Peter. "Optical Digital Recording." [In: National Archives of Canada. *Proceedings of Conservation in Archives. International Symposium, Ottawa, Canada, May 10-12, 1988*. Ottawa: National Archives of Canada, 1989.: 223-232.]

> The paper gives an overview of storing documents on optical media. Issues discussed include capacity, access time, cost, and system obsolescence.

Ward, Alan. A Manual of Sound Archive Administration. Brookfield, Vermont: Gower, 1990.

> This manual contains information on the preservation of recorded sound media. It includes lists of instructions on the care and storage of audiotapes and compact discs.

"White Paper: Strategic Technology Considerations Relative to the Preservation and Storage of Human and Machine Readable Records." [Prepared for the National Archives and Records Service (NARS) by Subcommittee C of the Committee on Preservation, July 1984] *Western*

Association of Map Libraries Information Bulletin. Vol. 16, no. 3 (June 1985): 312-324.

This paper summarizes Subcommittee C's recommendations for the accessioning, storage, and preservation of archival, machine-readable records. The committee recommended that NARS should preserve machine-readable records on archival microfilm. The paper gives no suggestions for preserving nontextual, machine-readable records, nor for preserving machine-readable records in their original form.

Appendix B

Glossary

Compiled by Tom Hall

ADPCM - Adaptive Differential Pulse Code Modulation. Differential modulation in which the prediction algorithm is adaptive to the signal.

AIIM - Association for Image and Information Management

aspect ratio - The width to height ratio of a T.V. picture

CCITT - Consultative Committee for International Telephony and Telegraphy. Part of the International Telecommunications Union. CCITT sets international communications standards.

CD-I - Compact Disk-Interactive. Compact Disk standard that includes CD audio, CD-ROM, still video graphics, and animated graphics. The standard defines how data is put on the disk.

cinching - The slipping of the tape when force is applied to a reel of magnetic tape.

contrast - The degree to which a character or feature is distinguishable from its background.

DBMS - Data Base Management System. The primary control software used in manipulating computer information files.

DCT - Discrete Cosine Transform. In a lossy compression scheme the DCT with sequential representation converts the image to the frequency components.

gray scale - A series of shades from white to black in computer graphics. The more levels of gray scale that can be handled, the more realistic an image can be displayed.

IGES - Initial Graphics Exchange Specifications is an ANSI standard graphics file format developed by the U.S. Air Force for 3D wire frame models.

ISO - International Standards Organization. Founded in 1947 to set standards in all fields, ISO is part of the U.N. and represents more than 75 countries.

JPEG - Joint Photographic Experts Group. A joint ISO and CCITT committee.

lossless - In the compression of visual data for image reproduction or transmission, lossless refers to the quality or ability to keep all or a very high percentage of the data, but at the expense of the amount of compression that is possible.

lossy - In the compression of visual data for image reproduction or transmission purposes, a lossy state results in the reduction of quality of the reconstructed image after decompression. Lossyness allows a high degree of compression but at the expense of quality.

noise - The unwanted data in an electronic signal.

Raster imaging - Representation of a picture image as a matrix of dots.

refreshing - The repeating or recopying of data or information at regular intervals.

resolution - The amount of graphical information that can be shown on a visual display. The degree of sharpness of a displayed or printed character or image.

scaling - The adjustment of values to be used in a computation so that the values and their resultant are within the range that can be handled by the process or equipment.

SGML - Standard Generalized Markup Language. Coded data used in document formats.

SNR - Signal-to-Noise Ratio.

SQL - Standard Query Language. A language designed to interrogate and process data in a relational database. There are many varieties incorporated into different software packages.

TEI - Text Encoding Initiative. Guidelines to allow the easy interchange of text between different sites through the use of common terminology and tags.

TIFF - Tagged Image File Format. A standard file format used to capture graphic images. TIFF stores images in a bitmapped (raster) format.

WORM - Write Once Read Many. A storage device that can be recorded once, erased but not rewritten.

Appendix C

WISPPR: Members of the 1991–1992 Program Planning Committee

Louis Pitschmann, Chair
Associate Director for Collection Development and Preservation
University of Wisconsin - Madison

Jim Danke
Newspapers and Serials Librarian
The State Historical Society of Wisconsin

Joe Jax
Director
University of Wisconsin - Stout

Hans Jensen
Director
Portage Public Library

Norma Jones
Director
University of Wiscons - Oshkosh

Ed Meachen
Director
University of Wisconsin - Parkside

Janice Mohlhenrich
Preservation Librarian
Marquette University

Karin Sandvik
Acquisitions Librarian
University of Wisconsin - LaCrosse

Kathy Schneider
Executive Director
Wisconsin Interlibrary Services

Virginia Schwartz
Humanities Coordinator
Milwaukee Public Library

Anne Tedeschi
Consultant

For more inforamtion about WISPPR services and/or membership information contact:

WISPPR
728 State Street, Room 464
Madison, WI 53706-1494

(608) 263-2773

Index